Understanding

Business Contracts

Practical books that inspire

Turning Your Business Around
How to spot the warning signs and save your business from failure

Setting up a Limited Company
How to form and operate a company as a director and shareholder

Accounting for the Small Business
Understand financial accounting and stay in control of your business

Going for Self-Employment
Enjoy the sense of achievement and satisfaction that comes from being your own boss

The Small Business Tax Guide

howtobooks
For full details, please send for a free copy of the latest catalogue to:

How To Books
3 Newtec Place, Magdalen Road,
Oxford OX4 1RE, United Kingdom
email: info@howtobooks.co.uk
www.howtobooks.co.uk

Understanding and Negotiating Business Contracts

Master the small print and get a better deal

Jon Rush

howtobooks

Published in 2002 by
How To Books Ltd, 3 Newtec Place,
Magdalen Road, Oxford, OX4 1RE, United Kingdom.
Tel: (01865) 793806. Fax: (01865) 248780.
email: info@howtobooks.co.uk
http//www.howtobooks.co.uk

British Library Cataloguing in Publication Data
A catalogue record for this book is available from
the British Library.

Cover design by Baseline Arts Ltd.

Produced for How To Books by Deer Park Productions
Edited by Peter Drew
Typeset by Anneset, Weston-super-Mare, North Somerset
Printed and bound by Cromwell Press, Trowbridge, Wiltshire

Contents

Introduction

How will this book help me?

This book will help you:

* understand the effect of the law on agreements you make with other businesses; and
* avoid the main legal pitfalls when you are negotiating agreements.

How do I know whether this book is suitable for my business?

This book concentrates on simple trading agreements between businesses – that is, agreements to buy or sell products or services. It does not cover agreements with consumers (i.e., individuals buying in a non-business capacity), where special rules apply. When it comes to negotiating, this book concentrates on *what* you should be trying to negotiate in order to protect your business, rather than issues like psychology or negotiating tactics.

Does it mean I will never have to use a lawyer?

There will always be some situations where the best course of action is to seek specialist help and advice. It doesn't have to cost the earth and this book will help you decide when you need it.

Anything else I should know?

As you would expect in a book about small print, we have had to include some of our own – so here goes:

- This book is based on the law of England and Wales at the time of publication. If you are looking at an agreement which is governed by Scots law or the law of any other country, the legal position may be different.

- If you are doing any of the following, be aware that, although many of the basic principles are the same, special rules apply which are not covered in this book:

  - buying or selling a business

  - buying or selling land (including premises) or negotiating leases

  - negotiating a franchise, agency or distribution agreement

  - negotiating contracts of employment.

- Remember also that this book can only give you a general idea of the issues that are likely to arise when negotiating contracts. It cannot cover everything and is not intended to be a substitute for detailed professional advice.

Finally, for ease of reading we have used the male pronoun. No sexism is intended.

1

Why Bother with Contracts?

It's easy to be put off by contracts. They're often long, boring and written in obscure language. And in the enthusiasm to do a deal, the terms of the agreement don't always get the attention they deserve. So it's important to understand what contracts are and why they're worth bothering with. If you know the risks you are running by not paying attention to contracts, it will be much easier to motivate yourself to get to grips with the actual terms of the agreement.

This chapter also looks at the typical life cycle of a contract and gives you an overview of the other chapters covered in this book.

WHAT IS A CONTRACT?

A contract is an agreement that creates certain legally binding rights and obligations. These rights and obligations can be enforced by a court.

For example, let's say you run a stationery supplies business. If you agree to sell a large consignment of envelopes to a shop, then you have a legal obligation to deliver the envelopes on time. The shop has a legal obligation to pay for them. If it refuses to pay, then you can go to court to demand payment. Equally, if you fail to deliver the envelopes on time and the shop needed them by a particular date, then it will have a right to withhold payment. It may even be able to claim damages for the late delivery.

No need for writing

Some people think that all contracts need to be in writing. In fact, it's perfectly possible to have an oral agreement. For example, if you accept an order from a customer over the telephone, it's quite possible that a legally binding contract has come into existence – even though there's no formal document that's been signed by both sides.

This could cause you problems if, for instance, you don't have enough stock to fulfil the order. Legally, you may already be obliged to give the customer what they have asked for and you will be in breach of contract if you don't deliver on time.

Presumptions about business agreements

It may be that when you spoke to the customer over the telephone, you did not intend that to be the final word on the matter. But unless you made that clear in the course of your conversation, you could find it difficult to persuade a court that there is no contract. The court will start from the position that business people intend to make legally binding agreements. Lawyers call this a 'presumption'.

Ignorance of the law is no excuse

It may seem unfair that a court will sometimes say that there is a contract when in fact, you never intended to make a legally binding agreement. But contract law is not really about fairness. The courts assume that business people know what they are doing and can look out for themselves. It's no use arguing that you didn't realise the consequences of your actions – ignorance of the law is no excuse.

* LATIN FOR "HARD CHEESE, MATE!"

RISKS OF NOT HAVING A WRITTEN CONTRACT

If you don't have your agreement written down, this can lead to a number of serious and potentially very costly problems:

- *Difficulty enforcing payment* – if you are the seller, it may be difficult to force the customer to pay up. It will be your word against theirs when it comes to proving what you agreed on as the price, or even whether you agreed on anything at all.

- *No right to compensation* – if you are the buyer, it may be difficult to obtain compensation from your supplier if things go wrong. This could mean you end up having to foot the bill to sort out any problems.

- *Unlimited legal liability* – if you are sued by the other side, you may have no means of limiting your liability to them. This could expose your business to a very significant damages claim.

- *Immediate termination* – if there is no requirement to give advance notice of termination, there will be nothing to stop the other side from pulling out without warning. This could

13

be very damaging if you have been investing heavily in order to cope with an expected increase in orders, for example.

- *Insolvency* – if the other side becomes insolvent, it may be more difficult to reclaim any money owed to your business.

- *Unnecessary disputes* – if it's not clear what each side is responsible for (because no one has written it down), there is much greater scope for arguing about it. This makes it more likely that both sides will end up facing each other in court.

- *Wasted insurance premiums* – if you have insurance, your insurers may not pay up if they discover that you have not tried to protect yourself against certain risks by means of a contract.

- *Unhappy investors and trading partners* – if your business loses out because it didn't pay enough attention to its legal obligations, it may make investors and trading partners think twice before dealing with you in future.

ADVANTAGES OF HAVING A WRITTEN CONTRACT

Some of the advantages of having a well drafted, written contract are:

- *Gives you peace of mind* – you know that if things go badly wrong, you have some legal protection against the risks outlined above.

- *Avoids unnecessary disputes* – a well drafted contract will set out clearly the rights and obligations of both sides. This cuts down on the scope for arguing about who is responsible for what, what they have to pay for and when they have to pay for it. These are among the most common causes of disputes between businesses.

14

- *Maintains goodwill* – if you ever decide to sell your business, the purchaser will expect to see formal contracts with your customers and suppliers. If there aren't any, the purchaser will say that it's impossible to make a proper assessment of the legal liabilities of the business or the value of the goodwill in the business. This will be his cue to start bargaining for a lower price – assuming he doesn't walk away from the deal altogether.

- *Keeps insurers and investors happy* – as outlined above, your insurers and investors will expect you to have proper contracts in place whenever you transact important business.

And so you see children, if the Pied Piper had got the people of Hamlin to sign a contract for his pest control services, everyone would have lived happily ever after... .

Think positive

You will get the most out of negotiating contracts if you see them not just as a necessary chore, but as a way of ensuring that the deal actually works for your business.

Often, businesses spend too little time thinking about how their relationship with suppliers and customers will actually function in practice. The tendency is to focus on what will happen if things go well, not what will happen if things don't go quite according to plan. The process of setting out each side's legal obligations in a formal contract often throws up commercial issues which neither side has thought through properly. This may add to the time it takes to do a deal. But it will be time well spent in the long run.

THE LIFE CYCLE OF A CONTRACT

This section gives you an overview of the life cycle of a typical contract.

Negotiations and standard terms

Before a contract can come into existence, there will usually have to be some negotiations. If it is an agreement for a fairly standardised product, the negotiations may be very short indeed. But if the work which needs doing is more complex, then more detailed discussions may well be necessary.

Chapter 2 explains how you can protect yourself against the legal pitfalls of negotiations. It also explains how to use standard terms and conditions effectively.

The Scope of Work

The Scope of Work is the part of the contract that sets out exactly what work needs to be done. It is one of the most important parts of the contract but is often overlooked. Chapter 3 explains what you should cover in your Scope of Work and Chapter 4 tells you how to build it into the contract itself.

The small print

Towards the end of the negotiations, there will normally be discussions about the detailed terms of the contract, including issues like termination rights, warranties, liability and other 'small print'. Chapter 4 explains what is meant by most of the clauses you are likely to come across. It also tells you what changes you should make in order to protect your business.

Finalising the deal

Once the small print has been agreed, both sides should be ready to sign. You need to make sure you do this properly – otherwise your contract may turn out not to be worth the paper it is written on. Chapter 5 tells you what to watch out for.

Problems during the life of the contract

Problems which can occur during the life of a contract include:

- the supplier fails to deliver on time
- the supplier's work is not up to standard
- the customer fails to pay on time.

Chapter 6 explains how you may be able to use the contract to your advantage in these situations. It also looks at:

- chasing late payments
- making changes to the contract
- going to court.

The death of a contract

If everything has gone according to plan, a contract will normally come to an end when the supplier has done his work properly and the buyer has paid him for it in full. But sometimes contracts come to an end prematurely.

For example, one side may have a right to terminate the contract by giving six months' advance warning to the other. This is discussed in Chapter 6.

Using lawyers

If you have bought this book then you are obviously intending to do a certain amount of work on contracts yourself. But that doesn't mean that you should never use lawyers. Chapter 7 tells you how you can make use of them in a cost-effective way.

QUESTIONS AND ANSWERS

Q. *I often take orders from customers over the phone. In my line of business, there's no time to negotiate detailed contracts. What am I supposed to do?*

A. There's no problem about taking down orders over the phone. The problem only comes if you accept the order. As soon as you accept it, then you are promising the customer that you will supply them. What if you haven't got enough product in stock?

   Ideally, you should say that you will send the customer a confirmation later that day, in writing. This will give you an opportunity to check your stock and whether you can deliver by the date the customer requested. It will also allow you to create a written record of the amount they ordered, the price and the delivery date, which you can then send to them. If you find you can't deliver what they wanted, then you should contact them straightaway and tell them – again, it's worth confirming this in writing.

   Having a written record will be important if the customer disputes the order or refuses to pay. Writing to them is also an opportunity to draw attention to your standard terms and conditions. If you are in a business where there isn't time to negotiate detailed contracts, then standard terms are the only way to ensure that you get legal protection for your business. This is dealt with in Chapter 2.

Q. *Is it possible to make legally binding agreements over the internet?*

A. Yes. You can make an agreement by an exchange of e-mails or by clicking on an 'I agree' button on a website. The courts will also accept computer records as evidence of an agreement, including electronic signatures (see Chapter 5).

Q. *I tried to get one of the firms I deal with to agree to a written contract but they refused. What can I do?*

A. You can't force someone to enter into an agreement if they don't want to. You could take your business elsewhere. If you'd rather not do that, there may be ways that you can still protect your position – to an extent.

Buyers
If you are buying from this firm, then you should create a written record of the amount you ordered, the price you negotiated and any key requirements, e.g. 'the components must not be more than 15.5 cm in length' etc. You should send this to the firm as a confirmation of your order. This will help if you get into a dispute about what you ordered or the price.

However, if you need a guarantee that this firm will be able to keep you supplied over a longer period, you should consider taking your business elsewhere. Under your current arrangement, the supplier could turn around at any moment and say that they are no longer prepared to supply you. This could cause problems if you are already committed to supplying your own customers with products obtained from this firm.

Sellers
If you are selling to this firm, then you can try to protect yourself by similar means, i.e. by confirming their orders in writing, so that you at least have a written record of the

products and the price. However, if the firm refuses to enter into a written agreement, there is no way for you to limit your business's liability if something goes wrong. You should consider carefully whether you are prepared to run that risk, (see section 11 of Chapter 4).

If you are heavily dependent on this firm as a customer, you should also make contingency plans about what to do if they suddenly stop ordering from you (see the case study on Baird Textiles below).

CASE STUDIES

The two real-life case studies below show how even very large businesses can come unstuck when they don't pay enough attention to contracts.

Baird Textiles

Some of the dangers of not having a formal, written contract are illustrated by a recent case involving a supplier of Marks & Spencer called Baird Textiles. Baird had been supplying M&S with clothing for 30 years. Sales to M&S were worth well over £100 million a year and accounted for 30–40% of Baird's total turnover. However, there was no formal, written contract between M&S and Baird. Towards the end of 1999, M&S suddenly announced that it was terminating the supply arrangement at the end of the current production season.

The courts ruled that there was no legally binding, long-term agreement between Baird and M&S. As a result, M&S was entitled to terminate the arrangement without warning, despite the fact that Baird had invested heavily over the years in order to meet its customer's needs.

This may seem very unfair to Baird. But as we have seen, the courts expect businessmen to be able to look out for themselves. Baird should have been aware of the risks it was running by not having a formal written contract with M&S.

What if there had been a proper contract?
The contract would probably have contained a term saying how much warning M&S had to give before terminating the agreement. This would have given Baird time to start looking for other customers to replace M&S or to cut back on its investment programme.

If M&S had insisted on terminating immediately, then it would have been in breach of contract. Baird could have claimed damages for the period from that date until the end of the contract notice period. If the notice period had been 12 months, for example, Baird could have claimed the value of a year's worth of business from M&S.

Equitable Life

The well-publicised case of Equitable Life shows how a bad contract can be just as bad as no contract at all, because you may be committing your business to something it cannot actually do. Equitable gave a commitment to certain policy holders that it would pay them guaranteed annual rates of interest. In the event, it didn't have enough money to do this.

Equitable tried to argue that it was not legally obliged to make the payments. The courts disagreed. They said that Equitable had entered into a legally binding agreement with its customers when it made the promise about guaranteed rates. If the promise later proved to be unwise, that was entirely Equitable's problem – its customers had a legal right to claim the guaranteed rates. Although Equitable is technically still solvent, it has now been forced to close to new business as a direct result of the contract it made with some of its customers. The Equitable case is an extreme example, but it shows the potentially disastrous consequences of failure to pay enough attention to contracts.

SUMMARY

* A contract is an agreement that creates legally binding rights and obligations and is enforceable through the courts.

* Having a well drafted, written contract will reduce your business's exposure to a wide range of commercial risks.

* BUT business people are expected to be able to look out for themselves when they make contracts, so it's vital to ensure that you don't commit your business to something it cannot actually do.

* Try to view contracts positively as a way of defining and managing the relationship between your business and its suppliers and customers – the best contracts are the ones that prevent you getting into a dispute in the first place, so you never need to go near a court.

2

Negotiating the Deal – the Legal Pitfalls

With some contracts, there may be a lot to talk about before the deal is done. You may have long meetings with the other side and lots of documents may fly back and forth. As we saw in Chapter 1, a contract can come into existence without having a piece of paper that's been signed by both parties. So how do you make sure that your business isn't committed until you're ready to do a deal?

In other cases, the scope for negotiation may be much more limited. You may receive a purchase order in the post with various terms and conditions on the back. All you have to do is agree to it and the deal is done. But can you afford to be legally bound by the customer's terms and conditions on the back of the purchase order?

These are some of the legal pitfalls of negotiating contracts which are dealt with in this chapter.

THE BASIC INGREDIENTS OF A CONTRACT

Before we look at the do's and don'ts of negotiating agreements, it's worth understanding the basic ingredients of a contract. These are the elements that a court will need to see before it can say 'Yes, a legally binding agreement has come into existence'.

When you are negotiating, you need to make sure that all these elements are present by the time you're ready to do a deal. Equally, if you're not ready to do a deal, you need to ensure that at least one of these elements is missing – otherwise there is a risk that a binding contract will come into existence.

The four main ingredients are intention, agreement, certainty and consideration.

The Naked Lawyer . . .

Intention

Both sides must intend to enter a legally binding agreement (but as we saw in Chapter 1, the courts assume that business people have this intention – so just saying that you didn't mean to make an agreement won't necessarily get you off the hook).

Agreement

The courts need to be convinced that one side has made a legally binding offer which the other side has agreed to accept. This is particularly important when you are dealing with standard terms (see below).

Certainty

If the terms of the agreement are vague or unclear then the courts will not enforce them (but there is no requirement for them to be written down).

Consideration

There will generally be no contract if one side promises to do something but the other side promises nothing in return. For instance, your customer must promise to pay you if he wants to be able to enforce your agreement, otherwise a court would say that he has provided no consideration.

NEGOTIATING DOs AND DON'Ts

Don't lose sight of the wider picture

It's easy to spend lots of time debating things like price that are bound to loom large in any negotiation. But don't lose sight of your other objectives. You should also be looking to make sure that your business is protected if something goes wrong. For example, it's no good having negotiated a fantastic price if you need the goods by a particular date but the supplier doesn't deliver on time.

So spend some time thinking about the other things which are important to you and make sure these are discussed in the course of your negotiations. Chapter 3 sets out many of the issues you may want to consider and ways in which you might deal with them in your agreement.

If your business is one where there is no time for detailed discussions with your customers about the terms of your agreement, then you should try to ensure that customers agree to your standard terms (see below under 'Dealing with standard terms').

Do mark your correspondence 'Subject to contract'

When you are still at the negotiating stage, make sure that you mark any documents you send to the other side 'subject to contract' – especially detailed documents like quotations and proposals. This is normally sufficient to make it clear that you do not intend to be legally bound until you have made a formal agreement.

OK guys, now before you go into the meeting I want you to slip
these T-shirts on . . .

But don't imagine that the phrase 'subject to contract' will give you a licence to say anything you like.

Do be careful what you say (or write)

Take care about what assurances you give to the other side, especially if they are in writing. It's all very well marking a document 'subject to contract', but if it contains important information that is incorrect, then it could cause you serious problems later on.

For example, the other side could claim that they decided to make an agreement with you because of a false statement you made in negotiations. They may be able to claim damages from you or walk away from the deal, even though they have signed a contract with you.

This may sound quite worrying at first – after all, you might say or write many things in the course of negotiations which could potentially be turned against you. But the courts are used to distinguishing between situations where someone has been seriously misled and situations where someone is just trying it on.

The key point is to avoid saying things like 'Yes, of course I can deliver it by the end of next month' when this timetable is unrealistic, or 'Yes, this product is suitable for use outdoors' when it may not be. It is this kind of statement that is likely to influence the other side to enter into a contract with you – and which could return to haunt you at a later date.

Do keep work to a minimum until you have a contract

Until you have a contract, there is no guarantee that you will be able to enforce payment for any work you do. If the customer walks away from the deal at a late stage of the negotiations, it may be difficult for you to get any money out of them for work you have done or investments you have made in anticipation of the deal going ahead.

Sometimes the commercial reality is that you will have to do some work before the contract is finalised in order to get the deal in the first place. If so, then you should try to keep that work to a minimum. Don't do it unless you're prepared to run the risk of not being paid should the negotiations collapse.

If you are the buyer, then this is not your problem. But it's worth bearing in mind that your supplier is likely to be more willing to get on and do the work once the contract has been signed – because the supplier then has an assurance that they will be paid.

Don't rely on heads of terms

Some people think that they have legal protection once they have agreed 'heads of terms'. These usually take the form of a summary of the main points of the agreement and are often signed by both parties. However, the courts will not usually enforce them. This is because it is normally clear that the heads of terms are not the final agreement. Normally, heads of terms that make it clear that neither side intends to be legally bound until they have drawn up that final agreement. For example, they often contain wording such as the following:

27

It is the intention of the parties, subject to negotiations, to enter into a formal and legally binding contract with each other for [*explain subject matter of contract*] on terms substantially similar to those set out in these heads of terms. However, nothing in these heads of terms is intended to be legally binding on the parties.

But heads of terms can be useful in other ways. They can help to crystallise the key points of many weeks of discussions. They also have a degree of psychological value. If one side has signed up to something in the heads of terms, it will make it more difficult for them to change their position later on in the negotiations. But don't put off finalising your agreement just because you've signed heads of terms.

Don't leave the detail of the contract until the last minute

Often, both sides put off looking at the detailed terms of the agreement until the last minute. In cases where the job needs to be done by a particular time, this can result in having to operate without a formal contract in place. This is bad news for both sides. The seller has no assurance that they will be paid and the buyer has no certainty about what happens if things go wrong (e.g. if the seller delivers late).

It is also possible that major disagreements will arise when it comes to negotiating the terms of the contract – over things that nobody had thought of in the earlier stages. So the sooner you can start negotiating on the detail of the contract, the better.

DEALING WITH STANDARD TERMS

Standard terms are useful where there isn't much time to negotiate over the detail of the contract. Where there is time to

Mr President, we don't have much time – so if you'll just sign these standard terms, I'll see what I can do about saving the world.

discuss the terms in detail, they also provide a useful starting point for negotiations.

Most businesses have standard terms of supply to cover contracts with their customers. Many larger businesses also have standard terms of purchase to cover contracts with their suppliers. The following assumes that you will be using standard terms mainly for contracts with customers.

Where to get hold of standard terms

Standard terms can be obtained from the following sources:

• commercial suppliers of legal documents (see Appendix 1)
• trade associations
• lawyers.

The trouble with the 'off the shelf' packages available commercially is that they won't be tailored to the needs of your business. If you are going to use one of these documents, make sure it is up to date and be very careful if you are selling to

29

consumers (see below). Read it through carefully to make sure that it really is suitable for your business. Chapter 4 will help you to make sense of most of the clauses you are likely to come across.

If you are a member of a trade association, it may be able to provide you with standard terms that have been specially adapted for your type of business. You may also want to consider getting your terms reviewed by a qualified lawyer.

This may seem an expensive solution. But think of the number of times you will be using your standard terms. And ask yourself whether you feel confident about relying on an 'off-the-shelf' product. Chapter 7 contains tips on how to find the right lawyer for you and how to keep the cost down.

Sales to consumers

A consumer is an individual who is not buying in a business capacity. If you are selling to consumers, you must ensure that your standard terms comply with special rules. For example, certain provisions which are acceptable in business agreements are not allowed in consumer contracts. They also need to be written in plain English.

If your standard terms don't comply with these rules, you won't be able to enforce them against consumers. If you are using an 'off-the-shelf' product, make sure it is up to date and has been drafted for use with consumers.

Drawing attention to your terms

Once you have got hold of some suitably drafted standard terms, you need to draw them to the attention of the other side. It is not enough to say that 'All sales are subject to our standard terms and conditions'. You need to actually send them your standard terms – and you need to do this before you supply them. The best approach is as follows:

- When you get a new customer, send them two copies of your standard terms, both signed by you.
- Ask them to sign both copies and return one of them to you.
- Do this *before* you accept any orders from them.
- Keep the signed copy from the customer in a safe place.

Assuming your standard terms have been properly drafted, then any future orders from the customer should now be subject to your standard terms. You should not need to get the customer to sign a new copy every time they contract with you (although if you can work out a procedure for this, then so much the better – see below).

You will, however, need a written record of what the customer ordered, the price and when they wanted it by, preferably signed by the customer. This will allow you to prove that the customer agreed to the order. You can do this by drawing up a simple 'confirmation of order' document with blanks for the relevant details. An example is given on the next page. But be careful about agreeing to customer purchase orders (see 'The battle of the forms', below).

Try to print your standard terms on the back of the 'confirmation of order' form and on delivery notes and invoices. On the front of each document you should include the statement 'All orders are subject to the terms and conditions printed overleaf'. This will give you extra protection in the event of any dispute about whether you brought your terms and conditions to the attention of the buyer. Do make sure that the print is readable.

Obviously, businesses where orders are taken down over the telephone will have difficulties with things like written confirmation. See the Case studies section at the end of this chapter for suggestions on how to deal with this.

The 'battle of the forms'

Take care if you receive a purchase order from the customer which refers to different terms and conditions from your own.

AARDVARK OFFICE SUPPLIES LTD
CONFIRMATION OF ORDER

IMPORTANT: ALL ORDERS ARE SUBJECT TO THE TERMS AND CONDITIONS SET OUT OVERLEAF

Order number:

Name of customer: (the 'Customer')

Address:

Tel: Fax:

Products:

Quantity:

Special requirements (if any):

Price (excluding VAT):

Delivery and other charges (if any):

Delivery date:

I confirm the order details set out above and accept the terms and conditions set out overleaf.

Signed _____

For and on behalf of the Customer

Please sign and return one copy to Aardvark Office Supplies Ltd of Unit 5, Collindale Industrial Estate, Filesden and keep one copy for your records.

Many larger businesses have standard terms of purchase, which are drafted to favour them as buyers.

If you receive one of these, you need to make it clear to the customer that you want the sale to be on your terms, not theirs. This is because the customer has rejected your original offer and replaced it with their own 'counter-offer'. If you accept that counter-offer, then you are agreeing to sell on the customer's terms, not yours. This is known as the 'battle of the forms'.

The battle of the forms

The best solution is to write back to the customer with a 'confirmation of order', which states that the order will be supplied on your terms. The customer should be asked to confirm that they accept this document.

Where the customer has signed and returned your terms and conditions, as suggested above, then the risk posed by the battle of the forms will be reduced – because well-drafted terms should allow you to argue that the signed agreement overrides any terms contained on the customer's purchase orders.

Amending standard terms

Sometimes customers won't like some of the provisions in your standard terms. Equally, you may not like some parts of your suppliers' standard terms. But this doesn't mean you have to walk away from the deal. It is perfectly possible to agree changes to standard terms. Chapter 5 tells you how to do this.

Chapter 4 will help you decide whether the changes being proposed are appropriate.

QUESTIONS AND ANSWERS

Q. *I put forward some changes to my supplier's standard terms but they refused to consider them. What can I do?*

A. Surprising as it may seem, many businesses are not used to having their standard terms questioned. The person you are dealing with may not even understand the terms or may be too junior to agree any changes. Try to get hold of someone more senior who can give your request proper consideration. If the answer is still 'no', then try the following:

- Make it clear that if they want your business, they need to address your objections to their standard terms.

- Work out which changes are most important to you and focus your efforts on them – the fewer, the better.

- Explain clearly what you are concerned about, preferably with examples.

- Put your objections in writing so that they can be forwarded to appropriately qualified staff or advisers.

- Ask for reasons why they can't accept your changes – this may help you find a compromise.

- Be firm but reasonable – show an understanding of the supplier's position as well as your own.

Q. *I am being asked to invest in new equipment and start supplying my customer before I have signed a long term supply agreement. I really want the business, but I am worried about operating without a contract. Is there anything I can do to protect myself?*

34

A. If you buy the equipment before you sign the long term supply agreement then you will be exposing your business to the risk of the customer walking away – leaving you with an investment you may not be able to use.

You may be able to give yourself some comfort by negotiating a short term, interim agreement with the customer, to cover the period between now and agreement being reached on the longer term contract. This will give you an assurance that you will be paid for the work you are doing in the meantime. However, the customer is likely to insist that the interim agreement can be terminated on short notice, so it will not give you much comfort over the longer term.

If you are not prepared to take the risk of investing without some form of assurance from the customer, then you could try to agree on what will happen if the customer does pull out. For example, in return for an improvement in your terms, the customer might be prepared to pay some of the costs of your investment if it pulls out before you have signed the long term agreement. You would need to make sure this was set out in your interim agreement in order to be confident of enforcing it.

If the customer won't agree to this, you will have to decide whether you are prepared to take the risk of going ahead with the investment without an agreement. Maybe you are reasonably confident that you can find customers elsewhere if this customer pulls out. If so, then the risk may be one which you can live with.

CASE STUDIES

Alicia's proposal

Alicia is a freelance interior designer. She drew up a detailed proposal for a business customer. The customer told her over the phone to go ahead with the work, so Alicia started ordering materials. The customer then changed its mind and claimed that it never made any agreement. It refused to pay for any of the materials. Alicia asked a lawyer if she could sue the customer to get back all the money she had spent. The lawyer said she could try, but she did not have very good evidence that there had been an agreement with the customer – all she had was her proposal, which the customer had never signed. As for the telephone call, it was her word against the customer's.

Before she starts work, Alicia now insists that all her customers sign a document which includes both her proposal, her fees, the cost of materials and her standard terms and conditions. The standard terms provide for the customer to pay for the cost of any materials and other expenses incurred by Alicia if they cancel the contract.

Bob's telesales problem

Bob runs a wholesalers selling electrical equipment and components to trade customers. Speed is key to his business: he promises next-day delivery. Most orders are taken by telephone. Bob has had to back down in a number of disputes with customers because he couldn't prove what they ordered or because no one had ever sent his terms and conditions to the customer (it was the word of his telesales staff against the customer). Since then, he has changed the procedure for telesales as follows.

• New customers are informed over the telephone that the sale will be subject to Bob's standard terms and conditions.

• These are sent to the customer by e-mail or fax as part of Bob's confirmation of order.

• The e-mail or fax states that the customer can cancel their order if they do not like any of the standard terms.

• The terms and condition are also reproduced on the delivery note, which tells customers that if they don't like any of the standard terms, they can send the products back free of charge

(Bob was nervous about this at first but has discovered that few customers take advantage of it).

- The telesales operators record themselves reading back the order to the customer together with the customer's response.

- The recording is stored digitally on computer using special software and can be retrieved easily in the event of a dispute.

Bob's solution is not quite as good as getting a signed copy of the standard terms back from the customer – but in the vast majority of cases, it should enable him to show that he brought his standard terms to the customer's attention and the customer accepted them by going ahead with the contract.

The software allows him to create a record of what customers have ordered. It was not as expensive as he had thought and works on a normal PC (for details, see Appendix 5). However, in order to comply with the law on recording telephone calls, he has to make sure that:

- His operators tell customers they are about to be recorded and explain what the recorded information will be used for (including whether it may be used for marketing purposes).

- Customers are asked to agree to the recording and the purposes for which the information will be used – if they do not agree, they must be allowed to withdraw.

- Only the part of the call confirming the customer's consent to the recording, the order itself and the customer's details is recorded – not the whole call.

- His company is properly registered under the Data Protection Act 1998 (see Appendix 5).

SUMMARY

- Don't lose sight of the bigger picture – make sure you get the necessary legal protection as well as a good price (see Chapter 3).

- Mark all correspondence 'subject to contract' until you are ready to do a deal.

- Be careful what assurances you give to the other side, especially if they are in writing.

- Keep work to a minimum until you have signed the contract.

- Don't rely on heads of terms.

- Don't leave the detail of the contract until the last minute.

- Make sure your standard terms are professionally drafted and are suitable for your business.

- Take sensible measures to bring your standard terms to the attention of customers and keep proper records.

- Beware of the 'battle of the forms'.

3

The Terms of the Deal – the Basics

Most negotiations do not start with a detailed discussion of the legal niceties of the formal, written contract. They start with a discussion of more practical issues like price or when the work needs to be done by. This is a perfectly sensible approach – even the most superbly drafted legal document will be of little assistance if you've made a bad deal in the first place. But it's also easy to spend too much time on one issue – usually price – at the expense of something which could prove equally important in the long run, like termination rights.

This chapter will help you to draw up a checklist of those fundamental issues and ensure that you do not lose sight of the bigger picture. At the end of it, you should be able to draw up a term sheet, like the example given below, setting out the key terms of the deal. This will help you in your negotiations and when you come to look at the detail of the contract.

Term Sheet

Parties: Aardvark Office Supplies Limited (customer) and KW Roofers Limited (supplier).

Description of work: repairs to warehouse roof – see attached for detailed Scope of Work.

Delivery dates/deadlines: 16 August 2002

Price and payment dates: £1,500 towards cost of materials on signature of agreement and £5,500 on completion of work to customer's satisfaction.

Warranties: Supplier to use all reasonable skill and care. See also specific standards in Scope of Work. Supplier to repair any problems occurring within 12 months of completion of work free of charge.

Duration/term: 12 August 2002 (projected start date) to 16 August 2002

Early termination rights: customer can terminate if supplier fails to complete work within two weeks of 16 August deadline (supplier to repay advance of £1,500 or hand over materials to customer).

WHO IS THE AGREEMENT WITH?

This may sound like a stupid question. Of course you know who the agreement is with. But how much do you know about them? Can you, for example, answer the following questions?

• What is the exact name and legal form of the business you are making an agreement with?

• Who owns it?

• Are its finances sound? Does it have the resources to pay you or do the work it is promising to do?

• Has it got the expertise to do this job?

• Does it have a good track record?

If you can't answer some of these questions to your own satisfaction, you may want to find out more about the other side before you go ahead. In some cases, that information may make you decide to pull out altogether. Alternatively, it may highlight issues which you will need to address in the contract.

For example, if you are buying from a company whose finances are shaky, you may be able to reduce the financial risk to your business by making sure that you only have to pay them once they have done their side of the bargain (see below under 'Price and payment').

WHAT WORK IS INVOLVED?

All too often, neither side spends enough time agreeing on a description of the work involved in the contract. If you are the buyer, this is important because it sets out what you want done and what work is included in the price. If you are the supplier, it is important because it sets out what work you need to do in order to get paid.

It may be easier to draw up the description of the work involved in a separate document, called a Scope of Work, which can be attached to the final contract as a schedule (see the next chapter). This document can be sent to and fro between the parties while they negotiate (but don't forget to mark it 'subject to contract' – see Chapter 2).

What to include in the Scope of Work

The Scope of Work does not have to be drafted in 'legalese'. The aim should be to describe what work is required clearly, in terms that both sides understand. Do not be afraid to state what you think is obvious. The exact nature of the Scope of Work will vary from one contract to another, but here are some guidelines about what to include:

• Briefly describe the purpose of the work.

• Describe the work to be done as fully as possible, including locations where the work is to be carried out (if relevant), materials to be used and so on.

• Include all quantities, measurements or other technical specifications.

• Make sure that any special or unusual requirements are clearly set out, e.g. where the products supplied need to be compatible with other products.

• If possible, include any minimum standards which the goods or services must meet, e.g. an official industry standard.

Here is an example – but remember each case is bound to be different. Another example is included in the Case study at the end of this chapter.

Scope of Work

Purpose of work: To repair leaks to roof of warehouse premises

Location: Warehouse premises at 14 Ringbinder Street, Filesden

Description of work: Repairs to leadwork on join between roof slope and right hand parapet wall (when facing warehouse outside main entrance) as follows:

- strip out existing lead flashing and arrange disposal
- fix new code 4 lead flashing
- render parapet wall as per diagram
- rendering to be carried out with 3–1 sand and cement mix including waterproof additive
- dress down new lead work
- liaise with customer's surveyor to arrange inspection of work when done.

DEADLINES

The contract should also set out when the work needs to be done by. If it is an agreement for the supply of goods only, then unless the goods are to be supplied in instalments, all you need is a delivery date which can be put into the contract. But if it is a more complicated project, you may need to draw up a timetable for completion of the work, with different dates for different stages of the work.

You also need to consider what happens if deadlines are missed. This will usually depend on the buyer's requirements, which are considered below.

Points for the buyer

- How easily can you find another supplier at short notice?

- If delivery is late, is it enough to be able to terminate the contract and get a refund of any advance payments?

- Have you negotiated very good terms? If so, you may want the supplier to pay for the extra cost should you have to look elsewhere (because you may not get such good terms elsewhere).

In some cases it may be difficult to find another supplier at short notice. If so, then terminating the contract may not be an attractive option. It is always useful as a threat, but it may be better to have some less drastic alternatives which deal with the problem in a more practical way. Possibilities include:

* Agreeing that, if deadlines are missed, the supplier will allocate additional staff and resources in order to get the work done as quickly as possible.

* Agreeing that, for every week that delivery is late, the supplier will give you a reduction in the price (this gives the supplier an incentive to deliver sooner).

Points for the supplier

* Are you confident that you can deliver on time?

* Is there anything the buyer needs to do before you can deliver?

* Can you live with whatever the buyer proposes should happen if you deliver late (see above under points for the buyer)?

PRICE AND PAYMENT

The contract will need to set out:

* how much is to be paid for the work; and
* when it should be paid by.

Points for the buyer

* Try to agree a fixed price for the work, most of which is payable only when the work is finished to your satisfaction.

* If you have to make some payments before the work is finished, make sure you can suspend payments if work isn't done on time.

- If the price is based on a daily or weekly rate, try to agree a fixed maximum figure for the cost of the work.

Points for the supplier

- Try to negotiate payment in instalments as work progresses, especially where you have doubts about the buyer's finances.

- Who pays if you go over-budget?

- If you are agreeing to do the work for a fixed sum, are you confident that you can do it at that price?

- Do you need money in advance from the buyer, e.g. to buy materials? If so, make this clear in the contract.

WARRANTIES

The contract needs to set out:

- what standards the supplier must meet (the warranties); and
- what happens if the supplier fails to meet these standards.

For a more detailed discussion of warranties, see section 10 of Chapter 4. Remember that, if the standards set out in the contract are not met, the usual remedy is financial compensation – so if you want the supplier to repair or replace goods which have developed faults, you will need to say so in the contract.

Points for the buyer

- What are the key standards the work needs to meet?

- As far as possible, have you set these out in the Scope of Work?

- What do you want the supplier to do if these standards are not met, e.g. should he be obliged to repair or replace any faulty goods?

Points for the supplier

• Is it clear what standards the buyer expects you to meet?

• Can you meet all the standards specified by the buyer in the Scope of Work?

• What does the buyer expect you to do if those standards are not met? Can you live with that?

TERM AND TERMINATION

The contract should set out:

• how long the agreement should last (the 'term'); and
• in what circumstances it can be brought to an end before that date.

How long should the agreement last?

A one-off supply contract will normally need to last until each side has fulfilled its obligations, e.g. the supplier has done the work and been paid in full. If, on the other hand, you have an agreement to supply goods or services on an on-going basis, with repeat orders, then you might want to consider the following possibilities:

• The agreement lasts for two years, but both sides can renew it for a further period of two years if they wish.

• The agreement lasts for five years but one side can terminate it after two years by giving six months' advance notice to the other.

• The agreement continues until one side tells the other that they do not want to continue, by giving six months' advance notice to the other.

There are many other possible variations on the above.

Points for the buyer

- How long will the contract last? Can you live with that? Do you need to be able to bring it to an end early?

- What rights does the supplier have to terminate the agreement early?

- Can you live with that possibility? If so, how much advance warning do you need from him?

- Try to make sure the supplier can't terminate until he has finished any work which he has already started or you have already paid for.

- If you terminate the agreement early, make sure you only have to pay for work already done.

Points for the supplier

- How long will the contract last? Can you live with that? Do you need to be able to bring it to an end early?

- What rights does the buyer have to terminate the agreement early?

- Can you live with that possibility? If so, how much advance warning do you need from him?

- If the buyer can terminate before the work is finished, make sure you still have a right to be paid for work done and costs incurred.

QUESTIONS AND ANSWERS

Q. *I have been negotiating with a company to construct a website for my business. I want to be able to terminate the contract if I am not happy with the results. My supplier won't agree to this – he says the way the website looks is too subjective an issue. What can I do?*

A. Your supplier has a point – if you put yourself in his shoes, you would also be worried by an agreement which allowed your customer to terminate the contract simply by saying 'I don't like what you've produced' and without giving any reason. However, there are ways around this problem.

The best solution is to agree on a detailed blueprint for how the website looks at the outset and include it in the Scope of Work. When it comes to more subjective aspects, such as the 'look and feel' of the site, think about suitable comparisons you could use to indicate how you want the site to look. For example, if the supplier has done other websites in the past, you could say that you would like yours to be of a similar overall 'look and feel'. If the supplier fails to meet these standards, then you can still terminate (assuming that is what the contract says) – but you will have to justify it in terms of the standards set out in the Scope of Work.

If you're not in a position to agree a detailed blueprint, the best approach may be to divide the contract into two stages; the first would be the design of the site and the second would be its construction. You would have an absolute right to terminate if you did not like the design produced at the end of the first stage. It may be that the supplier will want payment of at least some of their costs if you exercise this right to terminate early. But at least you will not be forced to proceed with something you are not happy with.

CASE STUDY

Harriet's web agreement

Harriet is manager of a stationery supplies business called Aardvark Office Supplies. The firm didn't have the expertise to set up its own website, so Harriet started discussions with a company called WebCo.

She had already drawn up a design of how each page of the

site should look, which WebCo was happy to follow. She explained that the site needed to be quick to download and she wanted disabled people to be able to access it easily. However, when Harriet received WebCo's terms and conditions, she discovered that they did not contain a proper description of the work. They simply referred to 'the Services' which were not defined. Harriet agreed the following Scope of Work with WebCo:

Scope of Work

Purpose of work: Aardvark Office Supplies requires a website to publicise its products and services. It has already produced a design for the site, which is attached to this Scope of Work.

Description of work: WebCo will produce the website, based on Aardvark's design:

- WebCo must produce a pilot version of the website (consisting of pages 1.1, 2.1 and 3.1 of the design) for approval by Aardvark before proceeding with the full version

- The website must conform as closely as possible to Aardvark's design

- If it is not possible to follow the design, WebCo must obtain Aardvark's agreement before proceeding with alternative designs

- The 'look and feel' of the website must be of comparable quality to WebCo's previous work on the website for Elephant Haulage Co (www.elephanthaulage.co.uk)

- The site must comply with the W3C standards on

---

accessibility by people with disabilities (see http://www.w3.org/WAI/)

- The site must download quickly, i.e. under normal conditions (as defined in the attached technical document produced by Aardvark's IT department), no individual page must take more than 15 seconds to download.

SUMMARY

Before you start looking at the terms of any contract in detail, make sure you have thought about the following:

- Who is your agreement with? Are you satisfied that they have a good track record and their finances are sound?

- What does the work involve? Have you drawn up a proper Scope of Work that sets out clearly what needs to be done?

- What is the timetable for getting the work done? What will happen if deadlines are missed?

- What is the price and what does it include? When does it have to be paid?

- What are the key standards that the supplier must meet? What happens if they are not met?

- How long will the agreement last? In what circumstances can it be terminated early?

4

The Terms of the Deal – the Detail

Your negotiations have been successful and it's time to produce a detailed contract for signature.

This chapter explains the main provisions you will be likely to come across in a typical agreement for the supply of products or services. It also explains how to make sure that the points you identified in the last chapter as being important to your business are included in the final, legally binding agreement.

Take time to go through the contract thoroughly before you sign it. If you need reminding why this is important, have a quick read of Chapter 1 again.

If you use the example wording from this chapter, please note the following:

- As far as possible, the various example clauses have been drafted so that they are fairly short and simple. In some cases, this means they may not give you quite the same level of legal protection you could achieve if you used a longer, more complex clause.

- You need to make sure that any wording you add makes sense in the context of the contract as a whole. Normally, you will need to adapt the example wording in this chapter to fit the particular definitions or terminology used in the contract you are reviewing.

The following checklist/clause finder will help you locate quickly the information you need on a particular subject.

Checklist/clause finder

1. THE DRAFTING PROCESS

First, some practical points about the process of actually drafting the contract.

The first draft

There are no fixed rules about which side is responsible for producing the first draft.

If you have your own standard terms and conditions, you may want to offer those as the basis of the contract, because they will have been drafted to favour your business. But it is no use just sending the other side your standard terms; you need to include things like the Scope of Work, deadlines, price and other matters discussed in Chapter 3.

Alternatively, you may be working with a contract drafted by the other side. You do not have to accept this document as it is. You can (and should) request changes to reflect what has been agreed in negotiations or to protect your business' position.

It is usual for each clause of the contract to be numbered e.g. 1,2,3 or 1.1, 1.2, 2.1, 2.2 etc, but there is no set way of doing this and you do not have to follow the order of the clauses in this chapter.

Making changes to the first draft

Where the contract has been produced on a word processor, it is a fairly simple matter to insert changes into the document. This is normally done by whoever produced the first draft.

If the contract is based on pre-printed standard terms, then it will often be easier to agree a list of modifications (rather than make amendments directly onto the pre-printed form). The final contract will state that the standard terms will apply, subject to the list of modifications. Chapter 5 explains how to draw up a document which achieves this.

2. PARTIES

The contract needs to identify who the agreement is between (the 'parties'). Normally, it will say something like:

This Agreement dated _____ is between

(1) Kevin Whitely, trading as KW Roofers, a sole trader whose principal place of business is at 5 Edgwick Gardens, Filesden (the Supplier)

and

(2) Aardvark Office Supplies Limited, a company incorporated in England and Wales whose registered office is at Unit 5, Collindale Industrial Estate, Filesden (the Buyer).

Why is it important?

Identifying the parties is crucial because without this, it is not clear who the agreement is between. A court will not enforce an agreement if it cannot identify who it should be enforced against.

The address given in the details of the parties may also be important if you need to serve a notice on the other side because you want to terminate, for example. See the part of section 16 below dealing with notices, page 109.

Points to check (buyer or supplier)

Always include the following:

- full correct name of the other side
- correct legal form of the other side (limited company, sole trader or partnership?)
- full correct address of the other side.

With limited companies it is normal to include details of the registered office. This is the address that the company has given to Companies House as the location for all official correspondence. Sometimes it will not be the company's business address but the address of its solicitors or other advisers.

With other types of business, such as partnerships or sole traders, it is usual to include the principal place of business, e.g. the head office.

3. RECITALS

Recitals set out the background to the agreement. Here is an example.

WHEREAS

(A) the Buyer owns a warehouse at 14 Ringbinder Street, Filesden, which is used for storage of all its stock (the 'Warehouse')

(B) the Warehouse is in need of repair because rainwater has penetrated through the roof, causing damage to the stock

(C) the Buyer's surveyor has identified the leak as being due to inadequate leadwork as detailed in the surveyor's report attached to this Agreement as Schedule 4

(D) the Supplier is an experienced roofer and has agreed to carry out the repairs to the roof specified by the Buyer upon the terms and conditions set out in this Agreement.

Why is it important?

The truth is that recitals are not always important. They are not the operative part of the agreement – they merely explain the background to it. However, they can be useful to set out why the agreement is important to one side or the other. For instance, in the example above the buyer has included:

- The circumstances that gave rise to the agreement (a leaking roof)

- Why it is important to have the work done (because the rainwater is damaging the stock)

- Why he chose the supplier (because he is an experienced roofer).

All these points could be helpful to the buyer if something goes wrong. For example, if the roof still leaks because the repair was not done properly and stock is damaged as a result, then the buyer may want to sue the supplier for the cost of replacing the stock. The supplier will find it difficult to argue that he wasn't aware that this damage could have occurred, because it is clearly set out in the recitals to the contract. Having said that, it is important to remember that recitals, although useful on occasions, are not essential.

Points to check (buyer or supplier)

You do not have to include recitals, but if you do, make sure that:

- they explain why you are entering into the contract and why it is important to you; and

- you can stand by any statement made about your business, e.g. that you have particular expertise or experience.

4. DEFINED TERMS

After the parties and recitals (if any), many agreements will have a clause setting out definitions of various words as they are used in the agreement. For example:

In this Agreement, the following terms shall have the following meanings:

'the Products' means the products described in Schedule 1
'the Services' means the services described in Schedule 2.

Defined terms referred to in the main body of the agreement usually begin with a capital letter, to make it clear that they have a special meaning.

Why is it important?

Sometimes a word may be ambiguous or unclear. Definitions may be needed to clarify what is meant. For example, it is not much help if an agreement simply talks about 'the products' — it needs to specify which products and how many of them.

Points to check (buyer or supplier)

- Don't look at definitions in isolation — check that you are happy with them by looking at the actual clause in which they are used.

- If you think you might need to come back to the definitions later, make a note of it so you don't forget.

- Don't try to define everything – if the normal English meaning of a word gets across what you want to say, there's usually no need to elaborate.

5. KEY OBLIGATIONS

The contract needs to set out:

- what work the supplier will do; and

- what the buyer will do in return.

The clause could be very simple, such as:

> In return for payment of the sums set out in clause [*refer to payment clause*], the Supplier will sell the Products/provide the Services to the Buyer on the terms set out in this Agreement.

Normally, you will need to define products or services in more detail. As suggested in the definitions section above, they could be defined in one or more schedules to the agreement. These schedules could be based on the Scope of Work document discussed in Chapter 3.

If you are entering into an on-going supply contract lasting say, two years, it may not be possible to describe the precise amount of products or the precise nature of the services, as this will depend on the buyer's order. Instead, you should include as much detail as possible and set out an ordering procedure (see page 61 under 'Points for the supplier').

Why is it important?

This clause is important because it contains an obligation on the supplier to do the work he has agreed to do. It also makes it clear that that he must be paid for doing it (although how much and when he will be paid is normally dealt with separately — see section 7, page 68 on price and payment).

As explained above, this clause will normally include a reference to a description of the work.

From the buyer's perspective, the description of the work is essential for holding the supplier to account; if the supplier has not done what he has promised to do, then he will be in breach of contract. What happens then depends on what the contract says.

From the supplier's perspective, the description of the work is important because it sets out what work he must do in order to be paid. If that isn't clearly described, there will be potential for a dispute over how much work was actually included in the price.

Points for the buyer

- Make sure the products or services are clearly defined and reflect your priorities.

- Consider referring to a schedule based on your Scope of Work (see Chapter 3).

- Make sure you have included any relevant quantities, measurements or other technical specifications.

- Try to include as many specifications as possible about the quality of the work.

Reflecting your priorities
The description of the work should reflect what is important to your business. So if it is essential that the work is done in a particular way, don't just assume that this is obvious to the supplier – say so in the contract.

Measuring the supplier's performance
Think about how you would use the description of the products or services to assess whether the supplier really has done what they promised to do. The more specifications you include, the better.

For example, if you have a contract for maintenance of computer equipment, it is no use just saying that the supplier will 'provide maintenance services'. You need to say what he will provide (telephone support only or on-site engineer?) and how quickly he will respond to your requests. Will he be obliged to use his best efforts to resolve the problem or will he have to replace the equipment if it can't be repaired? Who will pay if the equipment has to be replaced?

Points for the supplier

- Make sure the products or services are clearly defined and set out the limits of your responsibilities.

- Consider referring to a schedule based on your Scope of Work (see Chapter 3).

- Make sure you can live with any specifications included by the buyer, especially on quality – but don't be afraid of detailed specifications.

- Consider whether there is anything you need the buyer to do before you can carry out the work – if so, include this in the contract.

- If the agreement is for a long term supply with repeat orders, include an ordering procedure.

61

Setting out the limits of your responsibilities
As well as setting out what you will do as the supplier, it is sometimes helpful to say what you won't do. For example, if you are supplying maintenance services for computer hardware, it is worth making it clear that you are not responsible for problems caused by software or by other machines not covered by your agreement. This is especially important where the buyer might assume that those services are all part of the package and are included in the price.

Obligations on the buyer
Make sure you include anything you need the buyer to do before you can carry out your obligations. For example, let's say you are offering to install computer equipment. You would probably want the buyer to make sure that you had access to the location where the equipment is to be installed at the time you need it. You might also need one of the buyer's own IT staff to be on hand to help.

Ordering procedure
If the buyer will be ordering different amounts of the same products or services from you over a period of time, then obviously you cannot state the quantity that he will buy. However, you should make sure that you include an ordering procedure. This should cover:

• who can submit orders
• how they should be submitted
• when you will commit to fulfilling the order.

It is important to set out who in the buyer's organisation can submit orders because some people may not have the authority to do so. Ideally, orders should always be in writing so that you have a record of them. If the buyer wants to place orders by phone, then make sure your own staff have proper procedures for creating a written record of the call.

Finally, always ensure that you are only committed to

fulfilling the order when you have confirmed your acceptance of it to the buyer in writing. This will allow you to check whether you have sufficient products in stock and can deliver them by the time the buyer has requested.

6. DELIVERY

At a minimum, a delivery clause should set out:

• when the goods or services are to be supplied

• where they are to be supplied (if relevant).

It could be something very simple, such as:

> The Supplier will deliver the Products to [*insert address*] by [*insert time and date*].
>
> *Or, in the case of services:*
>
> The Supplier will provide and complete the Services by [*insert time and date*].

If the buyer has agreed to collect the products, then the clause might say:

> Delivery will take place by the Buyer collecting the Products from the Supplier's premises at [*insert address*] by [*insert time and date*].

The clause may also deal with what happens if delivery doesn't take place as planned. This is considered further below.

Why is it important?

The date of delivery is often important because it determines when the supplier gets paid — see section 7 'Price and Payment', page 68. If you are buying or selling goods, it may also determine when legal ownership of the products is transferred to the buyer — see section 8 'Risk and title', page 72.

But the most important feature of this clause is that it sets a deadline for the performance of the supplier's obligations. If he hasn't done what he promised by that date, then he will be in breach of contract. What happens then depends on what the rest of the contract says. See also the discussion of deadlines in Chapter 3.

Points for the buyer

* Are any delivery charges clearly stated in the contract?

* How important is it that delivery takes place by a specific date/time?

* What happens if delivery doesn't take place on time?

* Do you have to do anything before the supplier can deliver?

Delivery charges
Make sure any delivery charges are either included in the price or are clearly stated in the contract — otherwise you could find yourself paying more than you bargained for. See section 7 'Price and payment', page 68.

Time for delivery
If it is important that delivery takes place by a specific date, make sure the contract says:

64

> Time for delivery shall be of the essence.

This indicates that the deadline in the contract is especially important. Failure to meet it will normally mean that you can terminate the contract and seek damages for any loss suffered as a result of the late delivery.

It is also worth telling the supplier why you need the work done by a particular date and what you stand to lose if it isn't done on time. Try to document this in writing. Commercially, this may help to concentrate the supplier's mind on the importance of the deadline. Legally, it will help you if you need to claim damages for late delivery.

Failure to deliver on time
The supplier will normally resist being held to an absolute deadline and being liable for any losses resulting from late delivery. Whatever you agree, always ensure that the supplier won't get paid in full until he has delivered. This will give him a commercial incentive to get the work done.

If you are depending on the supplier to meet deadlines from your own buyers, make sure you can terminate the contract (and get a refund) if the supplier fails to deliver on time. Try to agree a date for delivery which gives you time to find another supplier if necessary.

Failure to deliver – whose fault?
With some contracts, the supplier may be depending on you to do certain things before they can deliver. For instance, he may need you to supply information about product specifications. These responsibilities should be clearly spelt out in the contract, otherwise there is a danger that each side will blame the other for the delay.

Many suppliers will also try to limit their liability for failure to deliver on time (see below under 'Points for the supplier'). Ideally you should try to persuade the supplier to remove this wording altogether. Other options are discussed in section 11 on Limitation of Liability (see page 86).

Points for the supplier

• Do you want to charge extra for delivery?

• Does the buyer need to do anything before you can deliver?

• Can you deliver by the agreed date?

• What happens if you deliver late?

Delivery charges
If you want to charge separately for delivery, you need to make this clear in the contract. See section 7 'Price and payment', page 68.

Buyer obligations
There may be certain things you need the buyer to do before you can deliver. For instance, you may need him to give you detailed specifications about the products or services by a particular date, otherwise you will not be able to deliver on time. These obligations should be set out clearly in the contract. Your obligation to deliver on time should be made conditional on the buyer complying with his obligations.

Time for delivery
If you have agreed a delivery date with the buyer, be aware that failure to deliver on time will normally allow the buyer to terminate the contract and claim damages for late delivery. The following wording should give you greater leeway when it comes to delivery:

> Time for delivery shall not be of the essence and all dates specified by the supplier for delivery of [the Products/ Services] are estimates.

However, the buyer may not agree to this. If so, there is no reason why you cannot agree on a specific delivery date provided you are confident you can meet it and take the consequences if you don't.

What happens if you deliver late?
If you say nothing about what happens should you deliver late, the buyer may be able to terminate the contract and/or claim compensation from you (for example, he may have lost business because you failed to deliver on time).

The following clause tries to strike a balance between the buyer and the supplier. If the supplier doesn't deliver, then the

> 3.1 The Supplier shall use its reasonable endeavours to deliver the [Products/Services] by [*insert date and time*] (the 'Delivery Date') at [*insert location*], but time for delivery shall not be of the essence. The Supplier shall not be responsible for any delay which results from failure by the Buyer to comply with its obligations under clause 3.3 below.
>
> 3.2 If the Supplier fails to deliver the [Products/Services] by the Delivery Date and provided that the Buyer has complied with clause 3.3, the following shall apply:
>
> (a) The Buyer may withhold any further payments under clause [*insert reference to payment clause*] until the [Products/Services] have been delivered; and
>
> (b) If the Supplier fails to deliver the [Products/Services] within [30] days of the Delivery Date, the Buyer may terminate this Agreement on giving [7] days' written notice of termination to the Supplier. The Buyer shall be entitled to a refund of any monies already paid for any [Products/Services] not delivered at the date of such termination.
>
> 3.3 [*set out what the Buyer needs to do before you can deliver*]

buyer does not have to pay – but he is only entitled to bring the contract to an end once delivery is more than, say, 30 days late. Whatever you agree, you should always ensure that your overall liability is limited (see section 11, page 86) and that you are not liable for a failure to deliver which is due to factors beyond your control (see section 13 on Force majeure, page 98).

You may want to add a further clause limiting your liability for late delivery. If so, you should be aware that it will only work if a court thinks it is reasonable. This is explained in more detail in Section 11 on Limitation of Liability, page 86, and Appendix 4.

> 3.4 The Buyer's only remedies for late delivery are as set out in clause 3.2. above and the Supplier shall not be liable for any loss (whether direct or indirect) caused by late delivery, (but nothing in this agreement shall limit the Supplier's liability for fraud or for death or personal injury caused by negligence).

7. PRICE AND PAYMENT

The price and payment clause needs to set out:

* how much is to be paid for the products or services; and

* when it has to be paid by.

For example, the contract might say:

> The Buyer shall pay the Supplier the sum of £[*insert amount*] by [*insert date*].

If the payment date is related to the date of delivery, the contract might say:

> The Buyer shall pay the Supplier the sum of £[*insert amount*] within [30] days of delivery of the Products/Services.

Alternatively, the clause could refer to a schedule of instalments, with different amounts due on different dates.

Why is it important?

If you are the supplier, one of the main reasons for having a written contract is so that it will be easier to enforce payment if the buyer doesn't pay on time. If you are the buyer, the payment clause is important because it sets out how much you have to pay and by when.

Points for the buyer

• Are VAT, delivery and any other charges included in the price?

• When do you have to pay? How much is due before delivery?

• What happens if you don't pay on time?

VAT, delivery and other charges
VAT will normally be regarded as included in the price unless the contract says otherwise. You should try to agree what the delivery charges will be and have them included in the price; that way, you know exactly how much you have to pay.
The following wording may be helpful if you are worried that the supplier might try to impose charges not written down in the contract:

> Unless otherwise agreed in writing, all expenses shall be borne by the Supplier and the only amounts payable to the Supplier shall be those set out in this agreement.

Time for payment
You need to make sure that you can withhold payment if the supplier:

• fails to deliver on time; or

• you are not happy with his work.

Failure to deliver on time is considered in section 6 above, page 65. Make sure that the supplier does not have a right to be paid in full until he has delivered in full. If you are not happy with the work that has been done, you will normally be able to withhold payment if you can show that he has not done what he promised.

You also need to be aware of what might happen if you don't pay on time. The supplier may be entitled to stop work or terminate the contract. This could be a problem if you need the work done by a specific time. The supplier could also take you to court and claim interest for every day that the payment is late. Often, the contract will specifically say that the supplier is entitled to claim interest, but even if it does not, he may well have an automatic right to do so because of recent legislation designed to combat late payment (see under 'Points for the Supplier' below). It is maybe worth adding the following wording to protect your position:

> Time for payment shall not be of the essence. If there is a genuine dispute over the Supplier's compliance with a material obligation under this agreement, the Buyer shall be entitled to withhold payment of all or part of the sums payable under this agreement.

Points for the supplier

• Does the price include VAT, delivery and other charges?

• When do you get paid?

• What happens if the buyer doesn't pay on time?

VAT and delivery charges

If the price is exclusive of VAT and/or delivery charges, then you need to say so:

> All amounts payable under this Agreement are exclusive of value added tax [and all transport and delivery costs], which the Buyer shall additionally be liable to pay to the Supplier.

Time for payment

If you are the supplier, it will be important to you that you are paid on time, so you may want to add:

> Time for payment is of the essence. If the Buyer fails to pay on time, then the Supplier may (i) suspend performance of its obligations under this Agreement; or (ii) terminate this Agreement immediately.

This will allow you to stop work or even terminate the contract if the buyer fails to pay on time. Both these rights can be used as 'threats' to encourage a buyer to pay up.

However, this wording is only helpful if you are being paid in instalments and if the buyer refuses to pay before the work is finished. If the buyer refuses to pay after you have finished the work, terminating the contract will not be much use. You should consider the suggestions in Chapter 6 on chasing late payments.

Bear in mind that, from 7 August 2002, all businesses will have the right to claim interest on late payments of the Bank of England base rate plus 8% (at the time of writing, this right only applies to businesses with 50 or fewer full time employees). The buyer can only exclude this right if the contract itself provides some other 'substantial' remedy for late payment. In practice, the best he can hope for is probably a lower interest rate e.g. base rate plus 5%. But don't try to make the buyer pay interest at a rate above base rate plus 8% because the courts probably won't enforce it.

8. RISK AND TITLE

Risk and title are only relevant where your agreement involves the supply of products. If it is for services only, then you can skip over this part. But if the agreement is for a mixture of products and services, you will need to deal with this point.

A typical clause dealing with risk and title might say:

> Risk and title shall pass to the Buyer on delivery of the Products.

What is risk?

Risk is a shorthand way of referring to who is responsible for the products if they are lost or damaged before delivery.

What is title?

Title refers to ownership of the products. Sometimes contracts also talk about 'property in the products'. This means the same thing as title.

Why is risk important?

Risk is important because it may affect what insurance you take out. For example, you might have a situation where your buyer says that he cannot take delivery of the products for one month, because he doesn't have enough storage space. He might ask you to store them instead.

What happens if your warehouse burns down the day before

the buyer is supposed to take delivery? Hopefully, you will have insurance to cover both the cost of the warehouse and any goods stored there. But you could decide to make the risk of loss of the products (not the warehouse) the responsibility of the buyer. This will mean that, as far as the products are concerned, it doesn't matter whether you had insurance, because they are being stored at the risk of the buyer, not you. It will be up to the buyer to arrange insurance for them. You might also want to charge the buyer for the cost of renting the warehouse space (if so, you will need to say this in the contract).

Why is title important?

If you are the buyer, you need to know when title in the products passes to you because you may want to sell them to other people or use them for your own purposes. If they are still the property of the supplier, you may not be legally entitled to do so.

If you are the supplier, you may want to prevent title passing until you have actually been paid using a so-called 'retention of title' clause. This has certain advantages which are discussed below.

Retention of title

Many standard terms of suppliers contain very long provisions known as 'retention of title clauses'.

The point of these clauses is to prevent legal ownership of the products passing to the buyer until the products have been paid for. The main advantage is that, if the buyer becomes insolvent, the supplier can demand the return of the products, because he still owns them. If the buyer has sold the products, then the liquidators of the company must hand over the proceeds of that sale. Crucially, they will have to pay out this money before they pay any of the buyer's other creditors, e.g. its banks, investors, shareholders and so on.

However, retention of title clauses have a number of disadvantages:

• They require expert drafting and you should always seek legal advice if you are planning to use them.

• In practice, many buyers will ignore what the clause says and it is difficult for suppliers to check up on them.

Points for the buyer

• Check when title and risk in the products pass to you (on delivery is the norm).

• If you need it, make sure you have insurance for the products from the time that risk passes to you, especially if risk passes before delivery.

• If you have to agree to a retention of title clause, remember that you will not own the goods until you have paid for them.

Retention of title clauses

As explained above, a retention of title clause means that you do not become the legal owner of the goods until they are paid for. However, you will normally be allowed to sell the goods — provided that you pay the money you received for them into a separate bank account. This is so that, in the event of your insolvency, the money derived from the sale of the products will be easy to identify. If you don't sell the products, you will be required to store them separately from your own property and insure them against damage.

However, it is doubtful whether many businesses pay much attention to these obligations in practice. It is also difficult for suppliers to check up on them.

Points for the supplier

- Check when title and risk in the products pass to the buyer (on delivery is the norm).

- If you need it, make sure you have insurance to cover the products until the time that risk passes to the buyer.

- If you want to use a retention of title clause, don't draft it yourself – seek legal advice.

Retention of title clauses
Retention of title clauses can be useful if the buyer becomes insolvent before you have been paid. But there are a number of practical problems with them and they require expert drafting (otherwise they risk being unenforceable). If you are concerned about the possibility of the buyer's insolvency but want to keep things simple, make sure you get paid in instalments, with as much of the money as possible being paid before delivery.

9. INTELLECTUAL PROPERTY

Intellectual property is ideas or information that are protected by law. It covers things like copyright, patents, trade marks, design rights and database rights. These are explained in more detail in Appendix 2.

If your contract is solely concerned with the supply of physical goods then you won't normally need to worry about intellectual property – so you can skip this section. But if the contract involves intangible products like computer software or services which will produce some intellectual property — such as a design for the interior decoration of an office or the text of a marketing brochure — then you will need to think about who is going to own that intellectual property. Will it be the buyer or the supplier?

If intellectual property is an important part of the contract, you should seriously consider getting specialist legal advice, since expert drafting will often be required. The following is only designed to help you think through the main issues.

Why is it important?

If you are the buyer, you need to make sure that you have the right to use any intellectual property which the supplier is offering. If not, you will risk being sued for infringing the rights of the owner of the intellectual property. In practice, there are essentially two options:

- the supplier transfers ownership of the intellectual property to the buyer (often referred to as an assignment); or

- the supplier remains the owner but gives the buyer permission (usually known as a licence) to use the intellectual property.

Licensing can be more advantageous for the supplier because he continues to own the intellectual property and can usually licence other people to use it — which allows him to make more money out of it.

Points for the buyer

- The best position is to own any intellectual property offered by the supplier — but this is not always possible.

- If you can't own it, make sure the licence gives you permission to do everything you are likely to need to do with the intellectual property.

76

- Get specialist legal advice if intellectual property is a major part of the contract.

Transfers of ownership

Let's say you have made an agreement with a design company to produce a marketing brochure for your business. That brochure will be protected by copyright, which will initially belong to the design company (because they created it).

For the purposes of your business, you need to be able to do what you like with the brochure without having to go back to the design company to ask permission all the time. The best solution is for the design company to transfer the intellectual property rights in their work to you. In order to achieve this, you need to make sure the contract contains wording stating that you will become the owner of the intellectual property rights in the brochure.

You should also make sure the contract contains a warranty from the supplier that:

- he owns the intellectual property; and
- the intellectual property does not infringe anyone else's intellectual property rights (e.g. it is not a copy of someone else's work).

Licences

If the supplier is unwilling to transfer ownership then you will need to obtain a licence from him to use the intellectual property. A licence of intellectual property is rather like a lease of a house; the house is not owned by you but you have the landlord's permission to live in it for a period of time in return for payment of rent.

Similarly, a licence of intellectual property such as software means that, although you do not own it, you have the owner's permission to use it – subject to certain restrictions. As the buyer, you need to ask yourself the following:

- What do I need to be able to do with the intellectual property?
- Does the licence give me permission to do all those things?
- How long does the licence last?
- Can I live with any restrictions imposed by the supplier?
- Am I happy about other businesses being able to use the same intellectual property — or do I need an exclusive licence?

For example, a software licence will usually only allow you to run the software on a certain number of computers. If you have 20 computers in your office but you also want to use the software on your computer at home, then a licence for 20 machines will not be enough.

If the intellectual property will give your business an edge over your competitors, you may want an exclusive licence. This means that the supplier will not be able to licence other businesses without your consent. If you are thinking of doing this, you should get specialist advice.

Points for the supplier

- The best position is to remain the owner of any intellectual property and licence it to the buyer.
- Make sure the terms of any licence impose appropriate limitations on what the buyer can do with your intellectual property.
- If the buyer insists on a transfer, make sure the intellectual property rights only transfer when you have been paid.
- If intellectual property is an important part of the agreement, get specialist advice on the drafting of the contract.

Licensing
The main advantage of licensing is that it allows you to make more money out of the intellectual property by licensing it to

other people. However, in some cases, the buyer may want to restrict the other businesses you can sell to on the grounds that your intellectual property gives him an edge over his competitors.

If you agree to such an arrangement, you need to know exactly who you can't sell to; this should be spelt out clearly in the contract. Commercially, you will probably want to raise your price to make up for the fact that you are prevented from selling to as many customers as before.

Appropriate limitations

If you are licensing intellectual property, you need to make sure that the buyer is not free to do exactly as he pleases with your property. You should consider:

- preventing the buyer from licensing the intellectual property to anyone else

- limiting what the buyer can do with the intellectual property to certain clearly defined purposes.

If intellectual property is an important part of your business, it is well worth getting professional advice on the drafting of your licence terms.

Transfers

If the buyer insists on becoming the owner of intellectual property that you have created, try to make sure that he will only become the owner once you have been paid. This is important because it gives you greater leverage over the buyer if he doesn't pay on time; unless he pays up, he will not have the right to use the intellectual property (because it will still be yours).

10. WARRANTIES AND INDEMNITIES

A warranty is usually a promise that the products or services will meet a certain standard. If they fall below that standard then the buyer will normally be able to sue the supplier. If there is a very serious breach of contract, then the buyer may even be able to reject the goods and claim his money back. A typical general warranty in a contract for the sale of goods would be as follows:

> The Products shall be of satisfactory quality and fit for their purpose. The Services shall be provided with reasonable skill and care.

As mentioned in Chapter 3, it is likely that there will also be some warranties contained in the Scope of Work, e.g. requirements that certain specific standards must be met.

An indemnity usually goes further than a warranty. It is normally a promise by the supplier to compensate the buyer if there is a breach of warranty. A typical indemnity in a contract for the sale of goods might be as follows:

> The Supplier shall indemnify the Buyer against all loss, damages, cost and expenses awarded against or incurred by the Buyer in connection with defective workmanship, quality or materials.

The pros and cons of indemnities are discussed under 'Points for the buyer' below.

Why is it important?

Warranties and indemnities are important for the buyer because they set out the standard that the supplier has to meet. If the required standards are unclear or are not very demanding, the buyer may find it difficult to obtain compensation for poor performance by the supplier.

Warranties and indemnities are important to the supplier because if he fails to meet the required standards, the buyer may refuse to pay him. They also define the circumstances in which the buyer can sue him for compensation if the products or services are not up to standard.

Points for the buyer

- Check that you have included as many specific warranties as possible in the Scope of Work (see Chapter 3).

- Make sure that the contract also contains general warranties that you can live with.

- Is it enough to be able to sue the supplier if the goods or services do not meet the required standard?

- If you can get an indemnity, so much the better – but it is not the end of the world if you can't.

Specific warranties
The more detail you can include about the specific standards that the work must meet, the better. These should be included in the schedule containing the Scope of Work. It is always worth setting out what the purpose of the work is.

General warranties
You should also ensure that the contract includes general warranties about the quality of the products or services supplied. The following warranties will usually be implied:

- The Products must be of satisfactory quality and fit for their purpose.

- The Services must be provided with reasonable skill and care.

See Appendix 3 for an explanation of what these terms mean in practice. The supplier will usually try to exclude these (see below under 'Points for the supplier'). This may or may not work —.so to be safe, you are always better off having general warranties written down in the contract, even if you adopt the standard, implied warranties (as set out above).

You should also include a reference to the schedule where you describe the work to be done (which should contain a number of detailed, specific warranties). For example, you might say:

> The [Products/Services] must conform to all specifications provided by the Buyer, in particular the specifications set out in Schedule [refer to Schedule which includes your Scope of Work].

If you think you need a higher standard than 'satisfactory quality' or 'reasonable skill and care', you might consider the following:

> - the Products must be of the best design, quality, material and workmanship and fit for their purpose
>
> Or, in the case of services:
>
> - the Services must be provided with the highest standards of skill and care.

Other remedies
Normally, your main remedy if the supplier fails to meet his promises is to sue him for compensation. But sometimes

compensation may be low down your list of priorities if something has gone wrong. It may be more use to you if the supplier is obliged to take certain practical steps if the goods or services do not meet the required standards. These might include:

- a promise by the supplier to repair or replace any goods which develop faults within 12 months of the date of delivery; or

- a promise by the supplier to allocate additional staff or resources to the project in order to get it up to the required standard.

If you want the supplier to be obliged to take these steps, you will need to set them out in the contract.

Indemnities
See the introduction to this section for an explanation of what an indemnity is. An indemnity has two main advantages:

- depending on how it is worded, it may allow the buyer to claim more money from the supplier; and

- it may be possible to claim compensation from the supplier without going to court (the buyer can simply send a letter saying 'You have not complied with the agreement and as a result, I have lost £X, which you must now pay to me').

However, there are a number of disadvantages as well:

- In practice, the buyer will often end up having to go to court anyway because the supplier refuses to pay.

- Indemnity clauses require expert drafting and you should seek specialist legal advice if you want to include them in your agreement.

If you can get an indemnity from the supplier, then so much the better – but it is not the end of the world if you can't.

Points for the supplier

* Don't expect to get away with offering no warranties at all — but make sure you have set clear limits on what you are offering.

* Make sure you can live with any promises you are making about the standard of your work.

* Resist the inclusion of any indemnity clauses.

Exclusion of warranties

The ideal position for the supplier is to offer no warranties at all — but this is seldom possible in practice. Offering no warranties at all is not likely to go down very well with your customers either.

The problem is that, even if you say that you are offering no warranties in your agreement, the courts can still 'read in' minimum standards, depending on the circumstances. In practice, the minimum you should normally expect to get away with is the following:

---

* any Products will be of satisfactory quality and fit for their purpose; and
* any Services will be provided with reasonable skill and care

---

In some situations you may be able to get away with less (see Appendix 4 for a full explanation of the law on this point). But this is also the minimum that most customers will expect to see, assuming they know what they are looking for — so attempting to exclude them entirely may not be good for your business.

Whatever warranties your contract contains, you should always include wording along the lines of the following:

> **ALL OTHER WARRANTIES, WHETHER EXPRESS OR IMPLIED, BY STATUTE OR OTHERWISE, ARE EXCLUDED TO THE FULLEST EXTENT PERMITTED BY LAW.**

This makes it clear that the only warranties on offer are those written down in the contract. It may not always have the desired effect (because in certain circumstances, the courts can still read in warranties if they think that the ones you have provided are insufficient), but you lose nothing by including it.

It is best to put this wording in **bold** and/or capital letters so that it stands out – this makes it more difficult for the buyer to argue that he wasn't aware of it.

Required standards
You need to be confident that you can meet the standards required by the buyer. In particular, look carefully at any specific warranties included in the description of the work and make sure you can meet these. Try to avoid agreeing to warranties which go further than the usual implied warranties of satisfactory quality, fitness for purpose and reasonable care (see above under 'Points for the buyer').

If you are re-selling products which have the benefit of a manufacturer's guarantee, you should make sure that you are not giving the buyer a warranty that is a great deal more generous than the one provided by the manufacturer to you. You may want to include a clause along the lines of the following:

> The Supplier will use its reasonable endeavours to transfer to the Buyer the benefit of any warranty or guarantees given to it by the manufacturer of the Products.

If you are doing this, you should notify the customer of the terms of the warranty or guarantee offered by the manufacturer before they go ahead with their order. You may also want to consider the Contracts (Rights of Third Parties) Act – see section 16 below.

Be aware that you cannot put all the blame back onto the manufacturer if things go wrong – legally, it is your problem if the products are not up to standard and it will be up to you (not the buyer) to sort it out with the manufacturer.

Indemnities
The advantages of an indemnity from the buyer's perspective are explained above. As the supplier, it is not usually in your interest to agree to an indemnity and you should resist it wherever possible.

11. LIMITATION OF LIABILITY

A liability clause should set out:

* the maximum amount that one side will pay to the other in compensation if they have breached the contract; and

* the types of loss (if any) for which no compensation at all can be claimed.

Clauses dealing with liability are often in the same part of the contract as the warranties, under a heading 'Warranties and liability'. Typical provisions dealing with liability might say:

X.1 Subject to clause X.3 below, the total liability of each party for all claims made by the other party arising from or in connection with this agreement (whether in contract, tort (including negligence) or otherwise) shall be limited to [£   ].

X.2 Subject to clause X.3 below, neither party shall be liable for loss (whether direct, indirect, consequential or special) of profits, business, reputation, data or goodwill or for non-pecuniary loss.

X.3 Nothing in this agreement shall limit the liability of the parties for fraud or for death or personal injury caused by negligence.

This clause is drafted to limit the liability of both the seller and the buyer. However, you will often see clauses which only limit the liability of seller.

Why is it important?

This clause will be very important to the supplier because it attempts to limit the amount he might have to pay in damages to the buyer if he fails to do what he is supposed to do under the contract. For the buyer, this clause is usually important because it may put a limit on how much he can recover from the supplier in the same circumstances. In some cases, it may also be important to the buyer to limit his liability to the supplier (see below).

Points for the buyer

- Do you need to limit your liability as well as the supplier's?

- What kind of loss has the supplier tried to exclude liability for? Can you live with this exclusion?

- Is the supplier's limit of liability high enough?

Limiting your liability as buyer

Many contracts only contain provisions limiting the supplier's liability to the buyer and not vice versa. This is because there is much more that can go wrong on the supplier's side of the bargain. He or she is usually the one who has to carry out some work under the contract, whereas the buyer's main obligation will often be just to pay for the work.

However, there may be circumstances where the buyer will want to make sure that his or her liability to the supplier is limited as well. For example, if the supplier is going to be working on the buyer's premises and will leave his equipment there, the buyer could be liable if the equipment is damaged. A liability clause can be used to limit the amount that the buyer has to pay for such damage. If this is the case, then you should make sure that any limitation of liability applies to both parties, not just to the supplier (see above for possible wording). Remember that it is illegal to exclude or limit liability for personal injury, death or fraud, so always include wording such as that in clause X.3 above.

If, on the other hand, the main risk faced by the supplier is that you might not pay on time, then you probably don't need to worry too much about limiting your own liability.

Types of loss which may be excluded

You will often see a clause such as X.2 above which says that the supplier has no liability at all for 'indirect and consequential loss', 'loss of profits' and other categories of loss. This clause is designed to prevent you claiming any compensation at all from the supplier for the types of loss referred to.

For example, let's say you run a 50-room hotel. Your supplier has provided you with minibars for each room. Normally, you would expect to make a reasonable amount of money on drinks sold from the minibar. However, the minibars have a fault and don't chill the drinks properly. It takes three months to get proper replacements. Your loss is as follows:

- cost of replacing the minibars

- wasted management and staff time sorting out the problem

- loss of profits on sales from the minibars because guests haven't been able to buy chilled drinks from them

- loss of a number of regular business customers to other hotels in the area; and

- damage to your reputation as a quality hotel.

A well-drafted contract in favour of the supplier will normally try to ensure that you can only claim for the first bullet point, namely the cost of replacing the minibars. All the other loss is likely to be excluded – even though it may well make up the lion's share of the total cost of the problem.

The best solution is to delete the exclusion clause and simply agree a financial limit on the supplier's total liability (unless of course you want to limit your liability to the supplier in the same way). If the supplier will not agree to this, you have three options:

- Do nothing and hope that if you ever do need to make a claim, you can convince a court that the supplier's exclusion is unreasonable (sometimes there is a fair chance that it will be – see Appendix 4).

- Get insurance cover for the loss that you may not be able to claim from the supplier (see under 'Points for the supplier' below for a summary of the types of policy available).

- Get legal advice on the clause – sometimes the involvement of a lawyer can help you to negotiate an appropriate compromise with the supplier (see Chapter 7).

But even if there is no exclusion in favour of the supplier, it is usually difficult to claim for loss which the supplier could not reasonably have predicted. In the scenario above, for instance, you would probably only stand a chance of claiming compensation for the loss of customers and damage to your reputation if you had made it clear to the supplier that a fault in the minibars would result in this kind of loss.

Limit of overall liability
The liability clause will also usually contain a clause limiting the overall liability of the supplier to a specified amount. You should consider whether this limit is likely to be enough to cover the cost to your business if the supplier doesn't do what he is supposed to do. Make sure you factor in costs like wasted management time sorting out the problem (see the minibar example above).

If the supplier refuses to raise the limit of liability, your options are essentially as set out in the preceding section, i.e. do nothing, get insurance or get legal advice.

Points for the supplier

- Have you excluded liability for indirect and consequential loss, loss of profits and so on?

- Have you limited your overall liability to the buyer? Is the limit reasonable?

- Make sure you haven't excluded or limited liability for fraud or for death or personal injury.

- Do you need insurance?

Loss of profits, indirect and consequential loss, etc.
If possible, you should include wording such as that in clause X.2 in the example at the beginning of this section. This clause tries to cut down the types of loss which the buyer can claim compensation for, should you breach your obligations under the contract. There is always a risk that this exclusion may not be regarded as reasonable by a court – in which case it will not

90

work (see Appendix 4 for an explanation of the law on this point). But as a supplier, you lose nothing by putting it in.

Limit of overall liability
You should always ensure that the contract contains a limit on the total amount which you could be liable to pay to the buyer in compensation (see clause X.1 above). Naturally, you will want this limit to be as low as possible. However, beware of putting in too low a figure. It may be unreasonable – in which case a court could simply disregard it and your liability will potentially be unlimited. Remember that it will be up to you to convince the court that your limit of liability is reasonable, should it ever be challenged.

As a rule of thumb, a limitation of liability is more likely to be reasonable if it bears some relation to the level of damage that the other side might suffer if things go wrong. Many contracts try to limit the supplier's liability to the contract price. This may be reasonable if the contract price is a relatively high figure – but if the contract price is low, the damage suffered by the customer could easily exceed this amount.

For example, in a contract for the supply of carbon dioxide gas for fizzy drinks, a court recently ruled that a limit of liability of £500,000 (five times the annual value of the contract) would have been reasonable. Appendix 4 sets out in more detail the factors that the courts take into account when deciding whether a limit of liability is reasonable. Bear in mind that every case is different – there are no hard and fast rules here.

Fraud, personal injury or death
You are not allowed to exclude liability for fraud or for personal injury or death due to your own negligence. Make sure you include wording such as that in clause X.3 above, otherwise there is a risk that a court could disregard all the exclusions and limitations of liability in the contract.

Insurance

You may want to consider insurance to cover claims from customers or other people who could suffer loss if you make a mistake in the course of your business. The following types of policy are available for this type of situation:

* *Professional indemnity* – covers mistakes made when carrying out contracts or other activities related to your business, e.g. you fail to repair a computer system properly, resulting in a claim for compensation from the customer.

* *Products liability, products guarantee and products recall* – covers claims arising from defective products.

* *Public liability* – covers injury to third parties or damage to their property, e.g. whilst working on a customer's site, you injure a member of the public.

How much cover you need depends on what you do. For example, you are less likely to need public liability insurance if you are a graphic designer working from home (unless clients actually visit you at your home and could be injured there).

Appendix 5 provides details of some useful insurance websites. Make sure you explain to your insurance adviser exactly what you want the insurance for – otherwise you could end up with cover that is not suitable for your business.

If you have insurance, you may also need to notify your insurers of the terms on which you do business, particularly any exclusions or limitations of liability.

12. TERM AND TERMINATION

A termination clause should set out:

- how long the agreement lasts; and
- in what circumstances it can be brought to an end before the normal expiry date.

For example, a termination clause might say:

X.1 Unless terminated in accordance with clause X.2 or X.3 below, this agreement shall continue until [*insert date or event, e.g. completion of work etc*]

X.2 Either party may terminate this agreement at any time by giving [6 months'] advance notice of termination to the other party in writing

X.3 Either party may terminate this agreement with immediate effect if:

- the other party has breached any of its material obligations under this agreement and fails to remedy such breach within 30 days of receipt of a written notice specifying the breach and requiring it to be remedied; or

- the other party ceases or threatens to cease carrying on business, makes a compromise or arrangement with its creditors or becomes the object of winding up, dissolution, administration, receivership, bankruptcy or any similar insolvency-related procedures in any jurisdiction to which it is subject and is in receipt of a written notice of termination from the party wishing to terminate the agreement.

Why is it important?

A termination clause is important because:

- It sets out the right of the parties to bring the contract to an end if one party has breached its obligations or become insolvent – without such a clause, you could be tied into the contract in spite of the other side's conduct.

- If the contract is going to continue for some time, it sets out how much advance warning one side has to give the other if they do not want to carry on with the contract – without such a clause, you would have to carry on until the contract expired.

Points for the buyer

- How long should the contract last? Can the supplier terminate early? Do you need to bring it to an end early?

- Do you have a right to terminate if the supplier is insolvent or breaches the agreement?

- What should happen after termination?

Contract duration
Unless the contract is for repeat orders, it should continue until the supplier has completed providing the products or the services. The supplier should not have a right to terminate until he has done everything he is obliged to do (although understandably, he will usually want a right to terminate if you are in breach of your obligations).

If the contract is for repeat orders, you will need to agree how long it should last for before you have to renegotiate the terms with the supplier. If it is going to last several years, then it may be sensible for you to have a right to terminate early, by giving say, six months' notice in writing (see clause X.2 above). It is not in your interest to let the supplier terminate early in the same way, but you may have to concede this if you want to have that right for your own business.

Insolvency and breach

You should always ensure that you can terminate the contract if the supplier is insolvent or he is in breach of his obligations to you. The ability to bring the contract to an end if the supplier is in breach is an important commercial threat. You may need to use it if the supplier's performance is unsatisfactory.

Most clauses of this type say that you have to give the supplier an opportunity to rectify the problem. You do this by giving him a written notice that he is in breach. The notice will state that he has, say, 30 days to do something about it. If he fails to resolve the problem, then the contract will end after the 30 days have expired. If you think the supplier should be able to resolve most problems in less than 30 days, then you should press for a shorter period.

It is also sensible to include a clause in the contract dealing with how notices should be sent and when they are deemed to be received. This is dealt with in section 16 below.

You may also want to the bring the agreement to an end early if the supplier's business changes hands – for instance, if it is acquired by one of your competitors. If so, you should include the following wording:

> The Buyer may terminate this agreement by giving [14 days'] written notice to the Supplier if there is any material change in the ownership of the Supplier which the Buyer regards as detrimental to its interests.

After termination

There may still be 'unfinished business' between you and the supplier at the date of termination. For example, the supplier may have some of your property in his possession, e.g. documents you have supplied to help him do the work. If so, it is worth including a clause which requires these to be returned.

If you are likely to get another supplier in to do the work instead, you may also want to include an obligation on the old supplier to co-operate in relation to any hand-over. A possible clause might be as follows:

> On termination of this agreement, each party shall promptly return all property of the other in its possession at the date of termination and the Supplier shall co-operate fully with any third party nominated by the Buyer to provide the [Products/Services] following such termination.

In addition, there may be some provisions of the agreement which you want to continue after termination. Examples would be the warranties clause (see sections 10 and 11 above) and (if you have one) a confidentiality obligation (see section 16 below, page 111). You can make sure this is the case by including the following wording:

> Termination of this agreement shall not affect the continuing validity and enforceability of the following clauses: [*insert numbers*].

Points for the supplier

- How long should the contract last? Do you need to bring it to an end early?

- When can the buyer terminate the agreement? Can you live with that?

- What should happen after termination?

Contract duration
If the contract is for a one-off supply of products or services, then it should normally last until you have finished doing the work and been paid. You will not normally want to terminate the agreement before then unless the buyer is in breach or has become insolvent.

For example, if the buyer fails to give you the co-operation you need or fails to pay you on time, you may want the right to bring the contract to an end. You can do this by including the wording set out in clause X.3 above. However, the threat of termination is unlikely to be attractive if you have already done a lot of work (for which you may not get paid if you terminate).

If there will be repeat orders over a period of time, then the same points apply as are made under 'Points for buyer' above, below the heading 'Contract duration'. In particular, you may want a right to bring a longer term contract to an end if your circumstances change.

When can the buyer terminate the agreement?

The buyer will normally demand a right to terminate if you are in breach of the agreement. This may mean that he can terminate if you fail to get parts of the work done by a certain time – so look carefully at any delivery schedule. In addition, make sure that the buyer is only entitled to terminate if you are in 'material breach' of the agreement – he should not be able to take such drastic action if you have only committed a minor breach.

The buyer may also have a right to terminate the agreement where you have done nothing wrong at all – but it just so happens that the buyer does not want to carry on with the contract. You need to consider whether you can live with that possibility. If you are investing a lot of money in new equipment to meet the buyer's needs, it may not be acceptable for the buyer to be able to terminate the agreement at short notice. You should try to negotiate a longer notice period which would allow you time to adapt to find replacement customers or make other arrangements.

You also need to make sure that you will be paid in full for all work that you have done up to the point of termination (unless the termination is due to the fact that you are in breach). You can do this by including the following wording:

> Except where the Supplier is in material breach of this agreement, the Supplier shall, following termination of this agreement, be entitled to payment in full for all Products/Services already delivered on or before the date of termination together with all costs and expenses incurred in relation to Products/Services not yet delivered at the date of termination.

After termination

The same points apply as those made under 'Points for the buyer' above, i.e. you may need provisions to deal with:

- return of your property which is in the buyer's possession

- hand-over to another supplier nominated by the buyer (try to agree that the buyer will bear the expense of this); and

- clauses which may need to continue beyond termination (e.g. confidentiality clauses and payment clauses).

For possible drafting, see under 'Points for the buyer' above.

13. FORCE MAJEURE

'Force majeure' refers to things like 'acts of God' which can sometimes prevent the contract being carried out. A force majeure clause should set out:

- what happens if the buyer or the supplier cannot comply with their obligations because of an event beyond their reasonable control; and

* a list of events which are regarded as beyond the reasonable control of either party.

A simple force majeure clause might say:

> Neither party shall be liable for any failure to perform or delay in performing its obligations under this agreement due to circumstances beyond its reasonable control including (but not limited to) fire, flood, acts of God, war, civil commotion, terrorism, strikes or other industrial disputes and acts of government. If the period of default continues for more than 30 days, the other party shall be entitled to terminate this agreement immediately by giving written notice.

Why is it important?

If you are the supplier and you are unable to deliver on time because of a fire at your warehouse, then technically you are in breach of contract. However, the force majeure clause recognises that events like this are not necessarily your fault. It is important because it prevents the buyer suing you for breach of contract for as long as you are unable to deliver because of the fire.

If you are the buyer, then you probably stand to benefit less from a force majeure clause. There could still be circumstances where you would be glad you had included it, such as a strike by bank staff which means that your payment is delayed (putting you in breach of your obligations to the supplier under the payment clause of your agreement). But if you are the buyer, the most important thing to check is that the force majeure clause does not make it too easy for the supplier to get out of his obligations under the contract.

Points for the buyer

* What does the clause cover? Does it let the supplier off the hook too easily?

* Can you terminate the agreement if the delay in performance continues beyond an acceptable time period?

Coverage of the clause

Events like war, fire and industrial action are fairly standard in a force majeure clause, so it's probably not worth arguing about them. But sometimes suppliers will try to include events like failure of their own suppliers to provide them with goods on time.

This kind of 'get-out' clause does not give the supplier much incentive to manage his own suppliers properly. It also means that you may find yourself unable to terminate the contract for late delivery because the supplier can argue that it is not his fault. You should only agree to the inclusion of this kind of event in a force majeure clause where you are able to terminate the agreement relatively quickly (without any need for the supplier to be in breach) and will not have much trouble finding another supplier. If you want to make it more difficult for the supplier to put the blame on his own suppliers, then you should modify the force majeure clause as follows (new wording underlined):

Neither party shall be liable for any failure to perform or delay in performing its obligations under this agreement due to circumstances beyond its reasonable control <u>and outside the ordinary course of business</u> including (but not limited to) fire, flood, acts of God [*clause continues as before*]. . .

You may also want to amend any reference to 'strikes and industrial disputes' so that it reads 'strikes and industrial disputes (other than those involving the Supplier's own workforce)'.

100

Termination rights

Make sure that the force majeure clause gives you a right to terminate the agreement if the supplier is unable to carry out the contract. How long you should have to wait before terminating depends on what the contract involves. If it is time-critical, then you may not want to give the supplier more than a couple of weeks at the most. In contracts drafted by suppliers, it is not unusual to see periods such as 60 days – which may be unacceptable to you.

Points for the supplier

* Are you reliant on third parties (e.g. your own suppliers) to carry out the contract? Does the force majeure clause cover this?

* How long are you likely to need in order to rectify the problem? Will this be acceptable to your customer?

Reliance on third parties

A common situation is where a supplier cannot meet a customer's order because his or her own suppliers have failed to deliver on time. This may not be your fault, so you may want to extend the force majeure clause to deal with that situation. You can do this by adding the following to the list of events that is regarded as beyond your reasonable control (see the earlier example clause – new wording is underlined):

> [....acts of government and] any failure of a third party to comply with its obligations to provide goods and services to the parties which are necessary for the performance of this agreement. If the period continues [*clause continues as before*].

However, the buyer will be likely to resist this. He will

probably argue that it is entirely your problem if your supplier turns out to be unreliable.

Rectifying the problem
It may be that there are ways around the event which has prevented you complying with your obligations. Make sure that the buyer is only entitled to terminate the agreement after you have been given a reasonable period of time in which to rectify the problem. If you don't make provision for this, then depending on what the contract says, the buyer may be entitled to go elsewhere and you may lose the business altogether.

14. GOVERNING LAW AND DISPUTES

A governing law and disputes clause should set out:

• which country's law should govern the agreement; and

• what should happen in the event of a dispute.

A typical governing law and disputes clause would be as follows:

> This agreement shall be governed by the law of England and Wales. The parties submit to the exclusive jurisdiction of the English courts for the resolution of all disputes arising out of or in connection with this agreement.

However, sometimes you will see clauses which provide for resolution of disputes by arbitration or alternative dispute resolution. Both these procedures are designed to prevent any disputes ending up in court. A very basic arbitration clause would be as follows:

> This agreement shall be governed by the law of England and Wales. Any dispute arising out of or in connection with this agreement will be resolved by arbitration.

But you will often see longer clauses which specify whether any special rules will govern the arbitration, where it is to take place and who should be appointed as arbitrator.

Why is it important?

If the agreement does not state which law governs the contract, the courts will not be certain which law they should apply. Just because your business is based in the UK does not necessarily mean that the English or Scottish courts will have the power to deal with any dispute or that English or Scots law will apply. In addition, if you want to use arbitration or alternative dispute resolution, you will need to say so in your agreement. These are explained in more detail below.

Points to check (buyer or supplier)

- Make sure the agreement states clearly what law should apply and which courts will resolve any disputes (unless you are using arbitration).

- Do you want to make use of arbitration or alternative dispute resolution?

Which law and which courts
This book is based on English law – so you should make sure that your agreement is governed by the law of England and

103

Wales and that any disputes will be resolved by the courts of England and Wales. Even if you are dealing with a business based in another country, there is usually nothing to prevent you both agreeing that English law will apply — indeed English law is quite commonly used in international contracts.

If you are being asked to sign a contract which will be governed by a different system of law (including Scots law), then you should seriously consider getting specialist advice from someone who knows about that system of law. This may also mean that you will have to sue the other side in the courts of another country, which could prove to be more difficult and expensive than suing in the English courts.

Arbitration
Arbitration is where both sides agree to appoint a single person to resolve their dispute, and to abide by his decision.

Advantages of arbitration include:

• more flexible procedure

• hearings are usually in private (avoids bad publicity)

• arbitrator can be someone with particular expertise in the subject (as opposed to a judge, who should know about the law but may have little technical knowledge).

However, arbitration is often no cheaper than going to court because both sides are usually legally represented and the procedure is still quite formal. It can sometimes be more expensive because unlike a judge, who is paid by the state, both sides have to find the money to pay the arbitrator's fees themselves.

It is also not possible to join third parties to the proceedings. For example, let's say you are being sued by a customer for supplying defective hi-fi equipment, but you believe that the fault lies with the manufacturer, not you. In that situation, a court will normally allow you to join the manufacturer to the proceedings as a third party.

This saves the court time because, at the same time as deciding whether you should pay compensation to the customer, it can also decide whether the manufacturer should pay compensation to you. With arbitration, however, this is not possible – if the arbitrator said you had to pay compensation to the customer, you would then have to bring separate court proceedings against the manufacturer to recover your loss.

If you opt for arbitration, make sure the contract does not include wording which says 'The parties submit to the exclusive jurisdiction of the English courts. . . .,' because the whole point of arbitration is to avoid having to go to court to resolve disputes.

Alternative dispute resolution
Alternative dispute resolution (ADR) is another way of trying to avoid court. The main advantage over arbitration or court proceedings is a more informal and flexible procedure. However, unlike arbitration, it is doubtful whether you can force the other side to follow this procedure – in which case court proceedings may be the only way of resolving the dispute. So ADR will only work if there is willingness on both sides to make it work. The following clauses are suggested by the Centre for Effective Dispute Resolution or CEDR:

If any dispute arises out of this Agreement, the parties will attempt to settle it by negotiation.

OR

If any dispute arises out of this Agreement, the parties will attempt to settle it by mediation in accordance with the Centre for Effective Dispute Resolution (CEDR) Model Mediation Procedure.

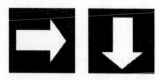

15. ASSIGNMENT AND SUBCONTRACTING

If you assign the agreement to someone else, you are transferring the benefit (e.g. the right to be paid) to them, but you remain legally responsible for any obligations under the agreement (e.g. work you are obliged to do in order to get paid). If you subcontract your obligations under the agreement to someone else, then you are effectively delegating your responsibility, i.e. getting someone else to carry out what you are obliged to do.

An assignment and subcontracting clause will set out whether you are allowed to either of these things — and just as importantly, whether the other side is allowed to do these things as well. An example clause is discussed below.

Why is it important?

If you are the buyer, it may be very important to you that the contract is actually carried out by the business you originally contracted with. For example, you may have selected that business for its expertise. The last thing you want is for the supplier to either assign the benefit of the contract to someone else or to make use of subcontractors without your approval.

Although legally, the supplier remains liable to you, he may have reached an agreement with the assignee (i.e. the person to whom he has assigned the benefit of the contract) or the subcontractor, which means that they will pay all his costs if he is sued by you. If so, then once an assignment or subcontract is in place, the supplier probably will not care very much how well the contract is performed – which is not good news for the buyer.

Equally, if you are the supplier, it may be important to you to have the flexibility to use subcontractors if necessary (but remember that legally, you are still responsible if the subcontractors do not do their job properly).

In addition, both sides may need the ability to assign the agreement – especially if there is a possibility that they will sell the business to someone else and the agreement could still be on-going.

Points to check (buyer or supplier)

* Do you want to prevent the other side assigning the agreement or subcontracting without your consent?

* Do you need to be able to assign or subcontract yourself?

Preventing assignment/subcontracting without consent
A typical clause of this type might say:

> The [Buyer][Supplier] shall not assign this agreement [or subcontract any of its obligations under this agreement] without the prior written consent of [*the other party i.e. the Buyer or the Supplier*].

If you need to be able to assign or subcontract freely, then you can just adapt this wording (replace 'shall not' with 'may' and delete the words 'without the prior written consent etc.').

16. OTHER CLAUSES

This section gives examples of typical clauses which you are likely to come across but which should normally be uncontroversial. They are usually found towards the end of a contract and may sometimes be grouped under the heading 'General' or 'Miscellaneous', together with clauses dealing with assignment and subcontracting and governing law and disputes (see above).

Entire agreement and variation

> This agreement constitutes the entire agreement between the parties. It replaces all prior agreements, representations and understandings between the parties concerning the subject matter of this agreement. No variation of this agreement shall be valid unless it is in writing, signed by all the parties to the agreement.

The aim of this clause is:

• to prevent one side claiming that something they said or did before the agreement was signed actually forms part of the agreement; and

• to ensure that any changes to the agreement are agreed by both parties and are recorded in writing.

But just by including this clause, you cannot avoid all liability for things you said or did before the contract was entered into (see Chapter 2 for a discussion of the sort of statement which may give rise to problems).

Notices

> Any notices given under this agreement must be in writing and sent by hand, by first class post or by facsimile transmission to the address below:
>
> - Notices to the Supplier: [*address, fax number*]
> - Notices to the Buyer: [*address, fax number*].
>
> Notices shall be deemed to be received as follows:
>
> - In the case of hand deliveries, on the day of delivery
> - In the case of first class post (properly addressed and with the correct postage paid), 2 days after posting
> - In the case of facsimile transmission sent before 4.30pm on a working day, on the day of transmission but otherwise on the next working day.

Most agreements contain provisions which may require one side to give the other 'notice' of their intention to do something. A good example is a termination clause, which will usually require one side to give the other advance warning that they are going to bring the agreement to an end. The other side may not want you to terminate. They may try to argue that you cannot do so because you have not served notice properly. This clause is designed to remove the potential for disputes of this type by specifying exactly:

- how such a notice should be sent; and
- when it is received.

In practice, the quickest and fastest way to ensure a notice gets through is to send a fax (assuming the contract allows this) and then put a copy in the post (make sure you keep a copy for your records, including the facsimile transmission report). This gives you two chances to make sure the message gets through.

The notice clause given above does not allow notices to be sent by e-mail. The main problem with e-mail is that, unlike faxes, by hand deliveries or recorded delivery, e-mail does not usually give you any indication of whether the notice has actually got through. If you are going to send notices by e-mail, you will need to:

- make sure the contract allows you to do this
- specify when the e-mail is deemed to be received (remember that e-mail is not always 'instant' – sometimes it can take hours to arrive)

As with faxes, it's usually best to print off a copy of the e-mail and put it in the post.

No waiver

> No waiver by either party of any breach of the other party's obligations under this agreement shall be regarded as a waiver of any subsequent breach of this agreement.

This clause is intended to cover a situation where, for example, you decide to give the other party more time to carry out their side of the bargain. It is known as a waiver, because you are not insisting on your rights under the contract. The clause simply makes it clear that in doing so, you are not giving up any of your other rights under the contract. This is not a 'must have' clause, although it is commonly used.

Severance

> If the whole or any part of any clause of this agreement is held to be invalid, the remainder of this agreement shall continue in full force and effect.

Sometimes the courts rule that a particular clause in an agreement is invalid and cannot be enforced. A good example is an unreasonable limitation or exclusion of liability (see above). This clause is intended to make it clear that, just because one clause is found to be invalid, the rest of the contract still stands. In practice, this is the approach the courts tend to adopt anyway, unless the clause which is invalid is so fundamental to the contract that the rest of the document makes no sense without it. So this is not necessarily a 'must-have' clause – although it is commonly used.

Confidentiality

> Each party shall treat as confidential all information obtained from the other by virtue of its relationship under this agreement except information which:
>
> - was rightfully in the possession of the party in question prior to the commencement of negotiations leading to this agreement; or
> - is already in the public domain or becomes public knowledge (unless as a result of breach of this clause); or
> - is trivial or obvious or otherwise of a non-confidential nature.
>
> Each party shall ensure that no such confidential information is disclosed to any person without the other party's prior written consent, except:
>
> - where required by law or regulatory authority; or
> - in the case of employees of the parties, where required to carry out the parties' obligations under this agreement (such employees to be informed on a need to know basis only).

This clause is intended to ensure that any information you give to the other side is kept secret – unless it is already public knowledge or is clearly of no value whatsoever. It is usually worth including if it is likely that the other side will obtain a certain amount of information about your business which you would prefer to keep secret. If you agree to such a clause, you are under a corresponding obligation to keep secret any confidential information which comes into your hands about the other side's business.

No partnership/agency, etc.

> The relationship between the parties is that of seller and buyer. Nothing in this agreement shall create a partnership, joint venture, agency or employment relationship between the parties.

This clause is intended to make it clear that the relationship between the parties is one of buyer and seller. It is designed to head off attempts by one party to argue that, despite what the contract says, they are in fact an employee or an agent, for example. One side might be tempted to argue this because employees and agents can sometimes claim special rights, which may enable them to claim more compensation in the event of a dispute. These types of relationships can also cause problems because they could result in your business being liable for things the other party has done or said without your knowledge.

This clause will of course be unsuitable if you are in fact entering into a partnership, joint venture, agency or employment agreement – and if so, you should seek further legal advice, since all of these raise important issues which are beyond the scope of this book.

Contracts (Rights of Third Parties) Act

> Nothing in this agreement is intended to create any benefits
> enforceable by third parties under the Contracts (Rights of
> Third Parties Act) 1999.

The purpose of this clause is to exclude the Contracts (Rights of Third Parties) Act. Until this legislation came into force, it was impossible for someone who was not a party to a contract (a 'third party') to sue one of the actual parties (i.e. the signatories) for breach of contract. So if you bought a computer from a retailer, you could not sue the manufacturer for breach of contract – because your contract was with the retailer, not the manufacturer.

Now that the Act is in force, it may be possible for you to sue the manufacturer direct for breach of contract, but only if the contract between the manufacturer and the retailer makes provision for this. In many cases, the parties do not want to give third parties the opportunity to sue them, so they specifically *exclude* the Act.

However, there may be situations where it is to your advantage for the Act to apply. For example, where you are buying products from a supplier which you will then sell on to another customer, you may want your customer to benefit directly from your supplier's warranties. If so, then you will need to agree this with your supplier. You may want to seek legal advice on the wording used to ensure that the Act applies.

5

Finalising the Deal

You have agreed the detailed terms of the contract and you are now ready to finalise the deal. This chapter tells you what to check before you go ahead and how to make sure the agreement is signed properly.

If your agreement is going to be based on standard terms, this chapter also tells you how to make changes to those terms without having to redraft the whole of the standard form agreement.

POINTS TO CHECK BEFORE YOU SIGN

- Does the contract contain everything that it should, e.g. are all necessary schedules attached, have all amendments been made?

- Does the contract make sense?

- Are the names of the parties correct?

- Is the person signing for the other side authorised to do so?

Making sure everything is included

When you sign a contract, you need to make sure that everything that is important to you is included in it – you cannot normally go back later and say 'Hang on a minute, I meant this document or this clause to be included as well'.

As discussed in Chapter 3, some of the most important parts of the agreement, such as the Scope of Work, may well be included as schedules. The terms of the main body of the agreement may make very little sense if these schedules are left out, because they often contain key pieces of information like the description of the work to be done.

You should also check that any amendments you wanted made have in fact been put in correctly, especially if those changes are being made by the other side. If any handwritten changes have been made, these should be initialled by both sides to show that they agreed to them (and that the changes were not simply added later, without agreement).

Does the contract make sense?

It is always worth having one last read-through to check that the final document actually makes sense (you would be surprised how many signed contracts contain glaring errors and omissions of this type). If some of the wording has been changed during negotiations, check that the new wording:

- is not contradicted by another clause elsewhere in the contract; and

- uses the same terminology or definitions as the rest of the contract.

Are the names of the parties correct?

This may seem an obvious point – but it is no use having an agreement with the wrong business or with a business which does not exist. A mistake here may mean that you cannot enforce the agreement against the other side.

Authority to sign

You should also check that the person who is going to be signing for the other side has authority to do so. This is discussed further in the next section on signature wording.

Signature wording

Strictly speaking, you do not need a signed contract for there to be a legally binding agreement. The advantage of getting a signature is that you will not normally be required to produce further evidence that the other side agreed to the terms of the contract. So whenever possible, you should try to get the agreement signed.

In terms of layout, try to ensure that at least some of the clauses of the contract run over onto the signature page. If you do not do this, then you make it easier for someone to commit fraud. For example, they could detach the signature page and attach it to another document that you never agreed to. You could also ask each side to sign their initials at the bottom of each page. This makes it more difficult for someone to insert additional pages into the contract which were never agreed.

Who should sign – and what wording you use – depends on the type of business involved.

Companies (including PLCs)
Any person authorised to do so can sign an agreement on behalf of a company and the company will normally be bound by their signature. That person need not be a director of the company – they could simply be a manager who has been given the power to sign agreements on the company's behalf. The signature clause in the contract would say something like:

> Signed by [*name of person signing*]_____
>
> ([*position e.g. director*])
> for and on behalf of [*name of company*]

If the person in question is not a director or a senior manager, it is worth querying whether they do in fact have power to sign. If they answer yes, make a note of their reply.

If you want to be absolutely sure that the company you are dealing with is bound by your agreement, you should ask for it to be signed by two directors or one director and the company secretary, as follows (but many companies will only do this for contracts above a certain value):

> Signed by [*name of person signing*]   _____
> for and on behalf of [*name of company*]   Director
>
>
> Signed by [*name of person signing*]   _____
> for and on behalf of [*name of company*]   Director/Company
>   Secretary

Sole traders (individuals)

If the business is a sole trader, then the signature of the individual concerned will be sufficient. So the contract would simply say:

> Signed by [*name of person signing*] _____

Partnerships

Agreements with partnerships should be signed by one of the partners, who will normally have authority to sign on behalf of the business as a whole:

> Signed by [*name of person signing*]   _____
> for and on behalf of [*name of partnership*]   Partner

Witnesses and electronic signatures are dealt with in the questions at the end of this chapter.

Getting the agreement signed

Normally both parties will sign at least two copies of the final agreement. This is so that each side has their own signed copy of the agreement.

If you and the other side can arrange to meet in order to sign the agreement, then so much the better. If not, then you should print out two copies and get them signed by the appropriate person in your business. Both copies should then be sent to the other side. They should be asked to sign both of them and return one signed copy to you.

Dating the agreement
Normally the date of the agreement will be the date that it is signed. If you have to send the agreement to the other side, ask them to insert the date on which they sign it.

If you want the agreement to start on a later date, there is nothing to stop you signing and dating the agreement on say, 25 September, but having a 'commencement date' of 1 October. You would simply add a clause which said:

This agreement shall commence on [*date*].

Strictly speaking, you cannot backdate an agreement, i.e. you cannot sign it on 25 September and say that the agreement is dated 1 September. But let's say you have already started work before signing the contract. There is nothing to stop you signing an agreement on 25 September and stating in the agreement itself that the contract covers work which started on 1 August. But don't take this as an encouragement to start work before you have a contract – you will regret it if you fall out with the other side before the contract is finalised (see Chapter 2).

Keeping the agreement safe

Make sure you keep the agreement in a safe place, where you can find it again. It's worth taking a photocopy of it and storing that somewhere different, just in case.

AMENDING STANDARD TERMS

Often, both sides are happy for the contract to be based on one side's standard terms, but the other side wants some changes to be made. Standard terms are often in very small type on a pre-printed form, so it may be difficult to amend them on the form itself. The simplest way around this is to draw up a separate document setting out the changes such as the one on page 120.

QUESTIONS AND ANSWERS

Q. Do I need to get someone to witness my signature?

A. No – not unless you are signing a deed (the type of contracts covered by this book will not normally be deeds). You will sometimes see signature clauses which require the presence of a witness, such as:

Signed by [*name of person signing*] _____
for and on behalf of [*name of company*] Director

in the presence of [name of witness]

Signed_____
[*Signature of witness*]
Address of witness

This is so that the witness can be called to give evidence if there is doubt about whether the signature on the contract is genuine. But there are other ways of dealing with a query about whether a signature is genuine, e.g. handwriting analysis. In practice, witness clauses tend to be used only in contracts which are particularly important to one side or the other.

This Agreement is made on [   ]

BETWEEN

(1) [   ] (the Supplier) of [   ]; and
(2) [   ] (the Buyer) of [   ]

1. This agreement is for the supply of [the products/services] set out in Schedule [1]

2. Dates for delivery and payment shall be as set out in Schedule [2]

3. The supply of the products/services shall be governed by the terms of [Buyer/Supplier] set out in Schedule [3] except for the following changes:

   - Clause [ ] shall be replaced with the following: [*insert text of revised clause*]

   - Clauses [   ], [ ] and [ ] shall be deleted in their entirety

   - Etc....

4. Any term of Schedules [1] and [2] which conflicts with Schedule [3] shall take precedence over the latter.

Signed by [*name of signatory*] _____

For and on behalf of [*name of business*]

Signed by [*name of signatory*] _____

For and on behalf of [*name of business*]

Q. Can I use an electronic signature?

A. Technically, yes – but in practice, it will often be easier and cheaper to use a normal, handwritten signature. Legally, anything you wish to use as an electronic signature can count as your signature. For example, you could scan your own handwritten signature into a computer. You could then send an e-mail with the text of the contract and your scanned signature (as a graphics file) as attachments and tell the recipient that they are to regard this as your electronic signature.

But there are a number of major security problems with this:

• someone else could detach the file containing your signature and start pretending to be you; and

• someone else could intercept your e-mail, change some details of the contract, and then send it back on its way.

So in practice, if you are going to use an electronic signature, you need one which encodes your signature (so someone else cannot use it). You also need one which alerts the recipient if the e-mail has been tampered with en route. That requires special software, which will cost a lot more than pen and ink. A further complication is that the other side will need the appropriate software and hardware to process your electronic signature.

So until electronic signature technology becomes more widely accepted, there is a lot to be said for pen and ink. If you are determined to use electronic signatures, Appendix 5 contains some useful sources of information.

Q. *Can I make an agreement by e-mail or fax?*

A. You can make an agreement by exchange of e-mails or faxes – there is no requirement for a signature of any sort, electronic or handwritten. The advantage of having a signature is that it amounts to very strong evidence that the other side agreed to what you were proposing. So it is always best to get a signature if you possibly can.

If the other side just wants to fax you their signature, ask them to put the hard copy in the post to you as well – then you have the signed original as well.

But if you have an e-mail or fax from the other side saying 'Yes, I agree to the terms you proposed in your last (e-mail/fax) and I want you to go ahead with the contract', this will normally be sufficient to amount to an agreement – despite the lack of a signature.

SUMMARY

- Check the agreement before you sign – make sure it covers all the points that are important to your business.

- Make sure the names of the parties are correct.

- Make sure the person signing it has authority to do so.

- Always try to get a signed copy of the agreement.

- Keep the agreement in a safe place!

6

What to Do if Things go Wrong

You have entered into a contract but something has gone wrong – perhaps your supplier has failed to do what you wanted, your customer is refusing to pay or you have realised that you cannot do what you originally promised under the contract. This chapter looks at how you may be able to use the contract to help you sort out the problem. It considers five possible courses of action:

- negotiating your way around the problem

- using the contract as a bargaining tool

- chasing late payments

- terminating the contract; or

- taking legal action.

NEGOTIATING YOUR WAY AROUND THE PROBLEM

In most situations, the best solution is to negotiate your way around the problem. This will usually be cheaper and quicker than taking legal action and will also help you stay on good terms with the other side.

For example, let's say you are the supplier and you realise that you are not going to be able to do the work on time. If you do nothing, you will risk not only annoying the customer but also breaching a term of the contract – which may entitle the customer to terminate and seek supplies elsewhere. But if you can persuade the customer to agree an extension then you should be able to avoid all these problems.

Always record your agreement in writing, preferably in a document signed by the customer. Many contracts say that variations are only valid if they are signed by both parties (check what your contract says). You can achieve this by writing a letter to the customer setting out the changes and signing two copies yourself. Send both to the customer and ask him to sign both and return one copy to you. Make sure the person signing on behalf of the customer has authority to do so. See page 125 for an example.

USING THE CONTRACT AS A BARGAINING TOOL

Not every problem can be resolved by a friendly chat with the other side. But before you start thinking about legal action, you should always explore whether the contract itself gives you the opportunity to bring pressure to bear.

Points for the buyer

If the supplier's performance is poor, consider writing him a letter pointing out the ways in which he has failed to comply with the contract. This shows you are aware of your legal rights and will sometimes be enough to make the supplier realise that you are not prepared to be messed about. Make sure you include the following:

- Identify the contract by subject matter and date.

- Specify the ways in which the supplier has failed to comply (include clause numbers if appropriate).

- Tell the supplier what you expect him to do and by when.

- Indicate what could happen if he doesn't do this, e.g. you will consider further action, including termination and/or legal action.

See page 126 for an example of the sort of letter you might write.

WebCo Ltd
12 Reed Avenue
Filesden

G Underwood Esq
IT Manager
Aardvark Office Supplies
6 Ringbinder Street
Filesden

17 September 200X

Dear Mr Underwood

Further to our discussion earlier today, I am writing to ask you to confirm the following changes to our contract dated 1 August 200X for design and construction of a website for your company:

- The deadline for delivery of the prototype of the website set out in Schedule 2 is extended to 5 October 200X.
- The specifications set out in Schedule 1 are modified as per the attached document.

I would be grateful if you would sign the enclosed copy of this letter and return it to me.

Yours sincerely

K Struthers, Managing Director
For and on behalf of WebCo Ltd

I agree to the changes set out in the above letter

Signed _____Date:_____

For and on behalf of Aardvark Office Supplies Ltd

Example letter: agreeing to change the contract.

Aardvark Office Supplies
6 Ringbinder Street
Filesden

K Struthers Esq
Managing Director
WebCo Ltd
12 Reed Avenue
Filesden

10 October 200X

Dear Mr Struthers

I refer to our contract with your company for supply of a website dated 1 August 200X (the 'Contract').

You were required to provide a prototype for the site by 20 September 200X (see Schedule 2 of the Contract). Despite numerous requests from our IT department, you have failed to provide the completed prototype. The material you provided on 5 October was incomplete and did not comply with our specifications as set out in Schedule 1 of the Contract.

We expect the completed prototype to be delivered to our offices by 9.00 am on Monday 15 October 200X. If you fail to do so, we shall be forced to consider what further action to take.

This letter is without prejudice to our rights under the Contract, including the right to seek damages from you and/or terminate the agreement for breach of contract.

Yours sincerely

A Renfrew
Managing Director, Aardvark Office Supplies

Example letter: using the contract as a bargaining tool.

You may also want to consider whether the contract allows you to withhold payments. The supplier will normally want to get his money – so this action may be enough to make him raise his game. But remember that you may put yourself in the wrong if you withhold payments without justification. You should always explain to the supplier in writing why you are withholding payment and what he must to do in order to be paid.

Points for the supplier

If the buyer is being unreasonable, e.g. he is expecting you to do more work than was originally agreed, it may be worth pointing out to him what the contract has to say on this. If the Scope of Work is properly drafted, it should support your case. This may be enough to get him to back down. In response to the letter given as an example under 'Points for the buyer' above, you might reply with a letter similar to the example on page 128.

You may also want to consider whether the contract allows you to stop work until the buyer does what you require. The buyer will normally want to get the work done – so this action may be enough to persuade him or her to be more helpful. But remember that two wrongs don't make a right – the buyer may be able to take you to court if you stop work without justification. Explain to the buyer in writing why you are stopping work and what he or she needs to do in order to make you start again.

Legal advice

If you are worried about the legal implications of stopping work or withholding payment, it may be worth getting legal advice on your proposed course of action. Chapter 7 explains how to do this without spending a fortune on legal fees. Sometimes, it can be worth spending money on a letter drafted by lawyers on your behalf because it may help to show the other side that you mean business.

WebCo Ltd
12 Reed Avenue
Filesden

A Renfrew Esq
Aardvark Office Supplies
6 Ringbinder Street
Filesden

11 October 200X

Dear Mr Renfrew

I refer to your letter of 10 October 200X. We believe that we have complied fully with the specification as set in Schedule 1 of the contract and have done all the work required to produce the prototype of the website. Attached to this letter is a detailed, point by point explanation of how the materials we provided on 5 October 200X comply with the specification in all respects.

We also dispute that we failed to meet the contractual deadline for delivery of the prototype. This was extended from 20 September to 5 October 200X by agreement with Mr Underwood, your IT manager, and confirmed in writing by him on 17 September 200X (a copy of his letter is attached).

We therefore consider that we have complied with all our obligations under the contract and would ask you to pay our invoice dated 5 October 200X without delay. In view of the above, I hope that it will not be necessary for you to consider further action. If there are any other matters you are unhappy about, please contact me direct so that we can discuss how they can best be resolved.

Yours sincerely

K Struthers

Example letter: using the contract as a bargaining tool.

CHASING LATE PAYMENTS

If you are the supplier and you have not been paid, you may want to explore the following options before you resort to court action:

• claiming interest on the late payment

• getting a solicitor to write a letter on your behalf; or

• using a collection agent.

Claiming interest

You may well have a right to claim interest on the debt of the normal bank base rate plus 8%, based on recent legislation designed to combat late payments. Appendix 5 tells you where you can find out more about this. It may be that a letter claiming such interest and setting out how much has mounted up already will encourage a recalcitrant customer to pay up – particularly if you offer to waive the interest if they pay within, say, seven days.

Using a solicitor

Solicitors will normally write debt-chasing letters on their firm's headed notepaper for a fixed fee. This may be cost-effective if you think the customer will be more likely to respond once lawyers appear to be involved (see Chapter 7).

Collection agents

Collection agents generally work on a 'no collection, no fee' basis and typically charge a percentage of the amount collected. Because they deal with this type of work all the time, they may be more effective at collecting the money.

TERMINATING THE CONTRACT

In some situations, the mere threat of termination may be enough to get the other side to comply with the contract. But if you are going to use termination as a threat, be careful what you say – especially if you are not prepared to go ahead with termination in practice. If the other side calls your bluff, you may be forced to back down, which could undermine your bargaining position.

In other situations, you may have decided that you want to get out of the contract – so it is not just a question of using it as a threat.

How to terminate

You do not normally need to go to court if you decide to terminate the contract. Usually, all you need to do is to send a written notice of termination to the other side.

But you must ensure that you are legally entitled to do this. Most contracts allow termination where:

* the other side has committed a 'material breach' of the contract (usually you have to give the other side a period in which to rectify the situation);

* the other side is insolvent; and/or

* one side gives a certain amount of advance warning to the other that they do not want to carry on with the contract.

But don't assume that your contract gives you these rights – look at the termination provisions of the contract itself.

Giving notice

Normally there will also be provisions in the contract which set out how much notice (or advance warning) you are required to give and how that notice is to be sent (e.g. by fax, by post, where to, etc.). These are discussed in section 16 of Chapter 4 – see page 109. If you do not comply with these clauses to the letter, you will not have terminated the contract properly. Here is an example of the sort of thing you might write if the contract allows you to terminate without giving a reason on 30 days' notice:

Aardvark Office Supplies
6 Ringbinder Street
Filesden

WebCo Ltd
12 Reed Avenue
Filesden

20 October 200X

Dear Sirs

**Contract dated 1 August 200X for supply of website between
Aardvark Office Supplies Ltd and WebCo Ltd ('the Contract')**

The purpose of this letter is to give you formal written notice of our
intention to terminate the Contract in accordance with clause 15. As
you are aware, clause 15 allows the buyer, Aardvark Office Supplies, to
terminate the agreement without cause on 30 days' written notice.

Yours faithfully

A Renfrew
Aardvark Office Supplies Ltd

Example letter: terminating by notice.

If you want to make use of the provisions of the contract which allow you to terminate where the other side is in breach, you will normally need to specify what breach has been committed. So you might write something like the example given on page 133.

There may also be circumstances where the other side has committed such a serious breach that you are entitled to bring the contract to an end immediately. But you should ideally consult a lawyer before you take such action – if the breach is not serious enough, you could be faced with a claim for compensation for unlawful termination (see below).

Risks of termination

Bear in mind that the other side may not be happy about the termination. They could take you to court to seek damages for 'unlawful termination'. They may also argue that you have not followed the procedures set out in the contract – so you have not in fact terminated the contract at all and are still under obligation to them. If in doubt, seek legal advice – see Chapter 7.

Termination may also pose other risks to your business. If you are the buyer, you need to consider how quickly and at what cost you can get someone else to do the work. If you are the supplier and you have not been paid, it may not be appropriate to terminate – because you may need to rely on the contract in order to enforce payment.

TAKING LEGAL ACTION

Taking legal action should be a last resort. You should always try to resolve the dispute by other means first.

Should you take legal action?

As with termination, the mere threat of legal action can

Aardvark Office Supplies
6 Ringbinder Street
Filesden

WebCo Ltd
12 Reed Avenue
Filesden

20 October 200X

Dear Sirs

Contract dated 1 August 200X for supply of website between Aardvark Office Supplies Ltd and WebCo Ltd ('the Contract')

The purpose of this letter is to give you formal written notice of our intention to terminate the Contract in accordance with clause 16. As you are aware, clause 16 allows the buyer, Aardvark Office Supplies, to terminate where the supplier is in material breach of the agreement by giving 15 days' written notice to the supplier specifying the nature of the breach. You have breached the following clauses:

Clause 5 (delivery): You failed to provide a prototype for the site by 20 September 200X, as required by Clause 5 and Schedule 2 of the Contract.

Clauses 4 and 10 (supply of services and warranties): Such material as has been provided does not comply with the specifications as set out in Schedule 1 of the contract, which you are required to meet by clauses 4 and 10 of the Contract (a detailed description of the manner in which the materials fail to meet the specification is attached).

Yours faithfully

A Renfrew
Aardvark Office Supplies Ltd

Example letter: terminating for breach.

sometimes be enough to get the other side to comply with the contract. But if threats don't work and you are seriously thinking about actually taking legal action, bear in mind the following points:

- It can be both time-consuming and expensive (even if you are not using a lawyer and are conducting the claim yourself, you will normally still have to pay court fees).

- If you lose, you will normally have to pay the other side's legal costs as well as your own.

- You need to be confident that the other side will be able to pay if you win – if their finances are shaky, you may never get your money.

On the other hand, if you have a strong case and the other side is likely to be able to pay the amount you are claiming, it can be worth taking legal action – and many businesses do so successfully every year. The Courts Service produces a useful leaflet called *Making a claim – some things to ask yourself* (Ref. Ex 301), which is available from your local county court or on the internet (see Appendix 5).

There are also a number of legal points you will need to consider before making your final decision:

Are you entitled to go to court?

First of all, check whether the contract allows you to go to court:

- Does the contract require you to 'escalate' disputes up to the senior management of the other side before you can take legal action?

- Does the contract say that any disputes are to be dealt with by alternative dispute resolution or arbitration rather than the courts?

- Does the contract say that disputes are to be dealt with in the courts of another country?

See section 14 of Chapter 4 for further discussion of these possibilities.

Time limits

There are time limits for taking legal action. For breaches of contract, the time limit is six years from the date of the breach. However, you may be able to bring other claims which are subject to a longer time period – seek legal advice if you are unsure.

What can you ask a court to do?

You can ask a court to:

- award you compensation (damages) because the other side has failed to comply with the contract

- order payment of sums that are owing to you under the contract, e.g. payment of the price or costs and expenses

- issue a declaration that you are entitled to do something under a contract

- order the other side to do something or refrain from doing something in order to comply with their obligations under the contract.

Most disputes involve the first two bullet points, which are considered further below. However, businesses sometimes go to court in order to resolve arguments over what the contract actually means. In these cases, they may ask for a 'declaration' saying whose interpretation is right.

In certain circumstances, it is possible to ask a court to order the other side to do something or refrain from doing something.

However, the courts will only do this where damages (i.e. monetary compensation) will not be an adequate remedy. In most cases, if a supplier fails to do what he has been asked to do, the court will not order him to do it – because the loss caused to the buyer can be compensated in monetary terms.

Claims for compensation

If your claim is for compensation, e.g. because a supplier has failed to do what he promised to do under a contract, you will need to produce the following evidence:

- A signed copy of the contract (if not, you will have to produce evidence that the other side did in fact agree to the contract, e.g. copies of letters which you wrote to them, copies of e-mails or notes of telephone conversations).

- Proof that the other side breached important provisions of that contract (this might take the form of statements from you, other people in your business or independent experts that various services or products were not provided in accordance with the contract).

- Copies of any correspondence regarding the breach.

- Proof that you have suffered loss as a result of the breach, such as receipts for the cost of repairing or replacing equipment and records of the amount of management time you have spent dealing with the problem.

You should try to produce as much documentary evidence as possible. Remember that the court needs to be satisfied that it should give judgment in your favour – so the more evidence you can produce which backs up what you say, the better.

Claims for non-payment

If your claim is for non-payment of money owed to you by the other side under a contract, e.g. your customer has not paid the purchase price, you will need to produce the following evidence:

• A signed copy of the contract (if not, you will have to produce evidence that the other side did in fact agree to the contract, e.g. copies of letters which you wrote to them, copies of e-mails or notes of telephone conversations).

• An assurance from you or from someone in your organisation that the debt has not been paid.

• Copies of any correspondence chasing the debt.

Remember that the other side may dispute that the money is owed. For example, they may say that they have not paid you because you failed to do the work properly in the first place – so be prepared to produce evidence to persuade the court that they are wrong. That evidence might take the form of statements from you, other people in your business or independent experts that the work has been done properly.

The courts service has recently launched a website called 'Money Claims Online' which allows you to start legal proceedings for recovery of debts over the internet – see Appendix 5.

Using lawyers

There is no obligation to use a lawyer – if you want to conduct the case yourself, you can. But it is likely to take up a fair amount of time and effort on your part. Using a lawyer will cut down on the time you need to spend on preparing your case. A good lawyer should also help you get a better result than you would be likely to achieve on your own. Chapter 7 tells you how to go about instructing a lawyer.

Making your claim

If you are not using a lawyer then you will need to visit your local county court to obtain a claim form and the accompanying guidance notes. You should also ask for a leaflet entitled *How to make a claim* (Ref. Ex 302), which will tell you what you need to do. This leaflet is also available on the internet (see Appendix 5).

You can ask court staff for help on how to fill out the form or explanations of the procedures involved – but they will not be able to give you legal advice on how best to go about it. Other leaflets are available covering the various different stages of your claim, which are beyond the scope of this book.

SUMMARY

- Always explore other options before you resort to legal action – if possible, try to negotiate your way around the problem.

- If you need to make changes to the contract, make sure you get the other side's agreement to those changes in writing.

- Use the contract as a means of bringing pressure to bear on the other side – draw their attention to the clauses of the contract you say they have not complied with.

- If you want to terminate the contract, read the termination provisions carefully and make sure you comply with any notice provisions.

- Think long and hard before you embark on legal action – especially if the other side's finances are weak.

- Make sure you have documentary evidence to support your case.

7

Using Lawyers

This chapter tells you how to go about finding a lawyer and how to instruct them in a cost-effective way. You might think about doing this if:

- you need to get some standard terms drafted for use in your business

- you are negotiating a contract with a customer or supplier

- you run into problems after a contract has been signed, e.g. the other side has failed to deliver on time or you have realised that you cannot do what you originally promised

- you want to terminate a contract

- you want to take legal action or someone is taking legal action against you.

WHY USE A LAWYER?

The main advantages of using a lawyer are as follows:

Peace of mind

Unlike this book, a lawyer will give you legal advice that is tailored specifically to the needs of your business – so you can have greater confidence that your business is properly protected.

Better use of your time

Drafting contracts or dealing with legal disputes can also be very time-consuming – it may well be that your time is better spent elsewhere.

Better results

When it comes to results, there can sometimes be a psychological advantage in having a lawyer acting for you, because it may make the other side take you seriously. But more importantly, a good lawyer will be able to advise you on how to draft your contract so that it is legally watertight. He or she will also help you make better decisions when it comes to dealing with disputes.

WHAT ABOUT THE COST?

The main disadvantage of using a lawyer is obvious – on the whole, lawyers are not cheap. Legal aid is only available in very limited circumstances (see 'Questions and answers' below).

But you should always weigh up the cost against the potential downside of not taking legal advice. For example, if your limitation of liability clause does not work, your business could be faced with a claim for hundreds of thousands of pounds if something goes wrong. Against that background, a certain amount of expenditure on legal advice may seem more justifiable.

This chapter also suggests some ways in which you can control costs when you come to instruct lawyers.

FINDING A LAWYER

There are a number of ways of locating a suitable lawyer:

* recommendations of friends or business colleagues

- *Yellow pages* or *Thomson Directories*

- the Law Society's *Directory of Solicitors*, available in libraries, on-line (see Appendix 5) or by telephoning the Law Society's Information Department on 0870 606 6565

- legal directories such as the *Legal 500* or *Chambers Directory* (available on the internet – see Appendix 5)

- the internet (an increasing number of lawyers now have a 'web presence').

Remember that lawyers generally specialise in particular areas of law. For example, if a firm specialises mainly in conveyancing, family law (e.g. divorces etc.) and criminal law, they are unlikely to be much help to you. You need a firm that acts for businesses and deals with commercial contracts on a regular basis.

MAKING CONTACT

Lawyers will not normally charge you for just ringing them up – but equally, you cannot expect them to give you legal advice for free.

If you are worried about being charged when you first make contact, raise it at the beginning of the conversation – explain that you are still making up your mind about who to instruct and you want to ask a few questions before taking your decision. Here are some points to consider for your first meeting or telephone call:

- Explain what you want and why you are thinking of obtaining legal advice.

- Make sure the lawyer you approach specialises in the type of work you want done, e.g. do they have much experience of drafting commercial contracts or contractual disputes?

- Ask about fees and say if you are not prepared to spend more than a certain amount (see below).

- If timing is important to you, ask how quickly they would expect to get the work done.

- Ask who will actually be doing the work – will it be the person you are speaking to or someone else at the same firm? Does that person have the relevant experience?

- Ask yourself whether you feel confident that the person you are dealing with can come up with a commercial solution to your problem.

What to look for

A common complaint about lawyers' advice is that it sometimes comes across like an academic legal textbook. But a good lawyer should be prepared to offer practical guidance as well an explanation of the legal position. So make it clear that you expect the advice to offer a commercial solution to your problem. But remember that you cannot expect lawyers to take your decisions for you – they are there to advise, not to decide.

FEES AND ESTIMATES

Lawyers should always tell you what their charges are before they start work and give an estimate of what the work will cost (they should confirm this in writing as well). If they haven't done so, don't be afraid to ask them.

Lawyers normally work on an hourly rate. Some lawyers will be prepared to work for a fixed fee when it comes to drafting contracts, for example – and you should always try to agree this if you possibly can. However, where the amount of work involved is less easily predictable, they will normally be reluctant to agree a fixed fee.

If I stop talking in mid-sentence, that means you
need to put more money into this slot.

Ways of keeping the cost down

If you cannot agree a fixed fee, there are a number of ways in which you can try to control costs:

* Give clear instructions – say what you want advice on, how you want it presented and when you want it by.

* Make sure that you have given your lawyer all the information he or she needs at the outset – you will end up paying more if significant changes have to be made to the advice because of something you did not tell them.

* Don't waste your lawyer's time – the longer they spend on the telephone to you, the more it will cost.

* Ask for regular reports on how much time has been spent and who has been working on the job – do not be afraid to query how time was spent.

* Make it clear at the outset that you are not prepared to spend more than a certain amount – ask to be notified as soon as costs are approaching say, 60% of this level.

* Make sure that time-consuming tasks are allocated to more junior lawyers (who will be cheaper) – but equally, make sure

143

that a senior lawyer has overall responsibility for the work and will be actively involved in supervising it.

If the estimate is too high

If the estimate given for the work you want done is too high, try to identify the areas you are most concerned about. See if the lawyers you have approached will agree to advise on those aspects alone.

For example, if the estimate for advising you on the drafting of the whole contract is too high, see if the lawyer will agree to advise you on a particular clause which you are worried about, e.g. warranties and liability. But remember that you will not be able to hold the lawyer responsible for any problems with the rest of the contract, because you are only asking him or her to advise on one part of it.

WHAT TO DO IF YOU ARE UNHAPPY WITH THE SERVICE

Try to sort out your problem with the lawyer you are dealing with first. Explain what you are unhappy about and what you want done about it. It is important to do this promptly and in writing (see below for time limits). Make a note of any telephone conversations and keep copies of all correspondence.

If your problem is still unresolved, then contact the Office for Supervision of Solicitors (helpline: 0845 6086565; address: Victoria Court, 8 Dormer Place, Leamington Spa, Warwickshire CV32 5AE; website: http://www.oss.lawsociety.org.uk).

Time limits

The following time limits apply:

• If your complaint is about a bill, you must complain to your solicitor in writing within 30 days of the date of the bill to activate the formal procedure.

- If your complaint is about something else, you must complain to the OSS within six months (if you leave it any longer, the OSS may decide not to investigate).

QUESTIONS AND ANSWERS

Q. *Can I ask a lawyer to take my case on a 'no win, no fee' basis?*

A. At the time of writing, 'no win, no fee' arrangements (also called 'conditional fee arrangements') were only available for cases involving personal injury, insolvency or human rights. Most disputes concerning contracts between businesses do not involve these issues.

Q. *Can I get legal aid?*

A. Legal aid will normally only be available if your income and savings are below certain thresholds. A solicitor or your local citizens advice bureau should be able to advise you. It is fairly unusual for legal aid to be granted in cases involving business matters.

Q. *My solicitor wants to instruct a barrister. Why should I have to pay for two sets of lawyers?*

A. Barristers (sometimes referred to as 'counsel') specialise in appearing in court on behalf of their clients – although they can also be asked to advise on the law more generally.

In the past, there was a rule that only barristers could appear in front of a judge – so solicitors had no choice but to use barristers if they were involved in a court case. Recently solicitors have been allowed to represent their clients in court. However, most solicitors will still use a barrister if they are involved in a court case.

Barristers generally have more experience of presenting cases in court – so a good barrister should help you get a better result. Going to court also takes a lot of preparation. It can sometimes be more efficient to divide up the work between the person presenting the case (the barrister) and the person who has done most of the day-to-day work on it (the solicitor). So the extent to which work is duplicated may be less than it appears at first sight.

Sometimes solicitors instruct barristers when they want a second opinion. Normally, they select a barrister who has particular expertise in that area of the law. In this case, you will be paying twice for what is essentially the same work – but this may be worthwhile if the second opinion helps you make a better decision about what to do.

Your solicitor should not instruct a barrister without your consent. You should ask him why he wants to involve a barrister and in particular, how much it is going to cost. If you are worried about duplication of work, raise this with the solicitor and ask for a breakdown of how time was spent. This should enable you to see whether there has been significant 'double work'.

CASE STUDY

Wasted money on good advice

Bob had been negotiating a five year exclusive contract with a new supplier of IT equipment. The contract was very important to his business, so he decided that it was worth spending some money on getting it reviewed by a firm of solicitors. A friend had told him that the best thing to do was to 'leave the lawyers out of it until the last minute – otherwise they'll only run up a hideous legal bill'.

Following his friend's advice, Bob approached solicitors fairly late on in the negotiations. They agreed to get back to him within a week with their comments. Their letter made a number of comments about the contract which Bob found quite worrying. They also included some suggestions about how the contract could be made more satisfactory. But when Bob tried to raise these with the supplier, he was told that it was now too late for major changes – if he didn't sign the contract now, the supplier would look elsewhere.

Bob realised that he had had made a mistake in leaving it so late to get legal advice – the money would have been better spent if he had involved lawyers at an earlier stage when there was still room for negotiation.

SUMMARY

- Using a lawyer should give you peace of mind, allow you to make better use of your time and get you a better result.

- When choosing a lawyer, make sure you get one who specialises in your area, e.g. drafting IT contracts etc.

- Always discuss fees before you instruct lawyers – if possible, try to agree a fixed fee rather than an hourly rate.

- When instructing lawyers, make it clear that you do not want an academic treatise on the law – you want a commercial solution to your problem.

- If you are unhappy with the service, don't be afraid to complain, just as you would about any other business providing a service.

Appendix 1

Obtaining Standard Contractual Documentation

A number of companies offer standard contracts and other legal documentation for a fixed price. Some of these are listed below. See Chapter 2 for guidance.

The details below are for information only. No recommendation is given as to the quality of the products and services provided by the companies listed below.

ContractStore Ltd
Address: 4 Middle Street, London EC1 7NQ
Telephone: 020 8241 1059
E-mail: feedback@contractstore.com
Website: http://www.contractstore.com/

CompactLaw Ltd
Address: 73 High Street, Abbots Langley, Hertfordshire WD5 0AD
Telephone: 01923 352789
E-mail: contact@compactlaw.co.uk
Website: http://www.compactlaw.co.uk/

Legal Services Shop
Address: New Premier House, 150 Southampton Row, London WC1B 5AL
Telephone: 020 7278 8888
Fax: 020 7278 1001
E-mail: enquiries@legalshop.co.uk
Website: http://www.legalshop.co.uk/

Lawpack Publishing Ltd
Address: Law Pack Publishing Ltd, 76–89 Alscot Road, London
SE1 3AW
Telephone: 020 7394 4040
Fax: 020 7394 4041
E-mail: mailbox@lawpack.co.uk
Website: http://www.lawpack.co.uk

*Note: all addresses and contact details were correct at time of
writing but may be subject to change.*

Appendix 2

Intellectual Property

The main types of intellectual property you are likely to come across are summarised below. Owners of intellectual property can go to court to stop others using that property without permission or without payment. See Chapter 4 for guidance.

COPYRIGHT

Copyright protects 'original works', including books, music, artwork, films and software. The protection lasts for the life of the creator plus 70 years. Copyright arises automatically when the work is created. There is no legal requirement to write the word 'Copyright [*Name of owner*]' on the work, although it is sensible to do this in practice.

PATENTS

Patents protect inventions (products or processes) which have a commercial application. The protection normally lasts for 20 years in the UK. Patents are only granted once the relevant authorities (the Patent Office in the UK) are satisfied that the invention deserves protection.

TRADE MARKS

Trade marks protect signs used to market goods or services such as logos or brand names. The protection lasts for as long as the trade mark is registered with the relevant authorities (the Patent Office in the UK). It is also possible to have unregistered trade marks. A court will protect unregistered marks if the owner can prove that they have built up significant goodwill in the mark (e.g. they have used it for some time in order to market their business).

OTHER INTELLECTUAL PROPERTY

Other forms of intellectual property you may come across are:

* Design rights to protect things like the shape of a product or its surface decoration.

* Database rights to protect things like an on-line directory of businesses.

FURTHER INFORMATION

The following government website contains a wide range of information about all the different types of intellectual property:

http://www.intellectual-property.gov.uk

Note: this address was correct at time of writing but may be subject to change.

Appendix 3

Satisfactory Quality, Fitness for Purpose and Reasonable Skill and Care

QUESTIONS AND ANSWERS

Here are some questions and answers you may find useful. You should already have read section 10, Chapter 4.

Q. What does 'satisfactory quality' mean in practice?

A. To be of satisfactory quality, products must normally:

- do what they are supposed to do
- be safe
- be free from defects, including minor ones
- function properly for a reasonable period of time; and
- have a reasonably satisfactory finish and appearance.

The first two conditions must normally be met whatever price the products are sold at. However, the standard of the remaining conditions depends on factors like the price of the products or whether they are new.

For example, if the products are second hand, it may be reasonable for the goods to last only a short time or have some defects, such as signs of wear and tear. If they are brand new, however, this will not be acceptable at all unless the defects have been pointed out to the buyer – who will normally expect a reduction in price to reflect this. Here are some examples – but remember that each case is different:

- A new Range Rover that was driveable but had a variety of minor problems with its engine and bodywork was *not* of satisfactory quality – especially in view of its luxury price tag.

- A second-hand car which had a defective clutch and broke down shortly afterwards *was* of satisfactory quality – because the seller had pointed out the defect and the price took account of it.

Q. *What does fitness for purpose mean in practice?*

A. Fitness for purpose refers to the products being suitable for the particular purpose that they buyer wanted them for. It only applies if the seller knew what that purpose was – or it was obvious from the circumstances. For example:

- The owners of a fishing vessel sued their suppliers when a camshaft broke. The component was of satisfactory quality and had only broken because of a peculiarity of the fishing boat it had been installed in. As the buyers had not told their suppliers about this peculiarity and it was not obvious, their claim failed.

Q. *What does 'reasonable skill and care' mean in practice?*

A. 'Reasonable skill and care' means that the services must be carried out with the same level of professionalism that a reasonably competent provider of those services would have used.

The standard assumes that the person carrying out the services knows what they are doing, although they are not expected to have above average levels of skill. For example, a person will not be in breach of their duty to use reasonable skill and care if they fail to do something that no reasonably competent provider would have done either.

Appendix 4

Excluding Warranties and Liability – What the Law Says

The law on exclusion of warranties and liability is complex and confusing. The following is designed to help you make sense of it. It is directed mainly at suppliers. You should already have read sections 10 and 11 of Chapter 4.

CONTRACT AND NEGLIGENCE LIABILITY

When you enter into a contract, two types of liability can arise – liability in contract and liability in negligence.

Liability in contract involves looking at what the contract says and working out whether the supplier has failed to comply with its provisions. Liability in negligence involves looking at whether there is a 'duty of care' and working out whether that duty has been breached. A supplier who has entered into a contract with a customer will generally owe that customer a duty to do what he has promised to do under the contract.

WHAT YOU CAN AND CAN'T EXCLUDE

The following points apply to contracts between businesses (stricter rules apply if consumers are involved):

- The implied warranties of satisfactory quality, fitness for purpose or reasonable skill and care can only be excluded in so far as it is reasonable to do so (see below).

- Where the contract is on the supplier's standard terms, limitations or exclusions of liability must also be reasonable.

- Where the contract is *not* on the supplier's standard terms, then the requirement for limitations or exclusions of liability to be reasonable does not apply. But a total exclusion is difficult to achieve in practice because you could still be liable in negligence (see final bullet point). The concept of 'standard terms' is also very wide and is often difficult to avoid, even where the agreement has been heavily negotiated.

- You can never exclude liability for personal injury or death caused by your negligence.

- Liability for other damage (i.e. not personal injury or death) caused by your negligence can only be excluded where it is reasonable to do so (see below). So even if a customer cannot sue you in *contract* (bullet point three), the chances are that they will still be able to sue you in *negligence*.

The practical upshot of the above is that it is generally best for suppliers to ensure that any exclusions of warranties or liability meet the test of reasonableness outlined below – even where they are of the opinion that the contract is not on standard terms.

FACTORS WHICH MAY MAKE A TERM UNREASONABLE

The courts look at a number of factors when deciding whether a term of a contract is 'fair and reasonable'. In practice, the courts will tend towards regarding a term as unreasonable if:

- the customer does not have much bargaining power and is in a weak position to negotiate improvements to the contract (but if the customer could easily have obtained better terms from another supplier, then the term in question is less likely to be unreasonable)

- the customer is expected to comply with some condition, such as notifying a claim within 10 days of delivery of the goods, and it is simply impractical to comply with that condition (e.g. because problems with the goods will only become apparent after 10 days have elapsed)

- the supplier is a large business with significant resources and is therefore in a better position to meet any claims from the customer; or

- the supplier could have obtained affordable insurance against the type of claim which the term is designed to prevent.

FACTORS WHICH MAY MAKE A TERM REASONABLE

Presence of the following factors may make it more likely that a clause will be regarded as reasonable (but not if they are outweighed by the factors listed above):

- In return for accepting a less generous limit of liability or less generous warranties, the customer has got a very good deal on some other aspect of the contract, e.g. a significant reduction in the price.

- The goods in question were made to the special order of the customer (in which case it may be more reasonable to expect the customer to bear some responsibility if things go wrong).

- The customer knew or ought reasonably to have known of the term, e.g. it is a very common term in the industry (although in practice, this factor rarely seems to be decisive).

- The supplier is a relatively small business which does not have the resources to meet a large claim and is also unable to obtain affordable insurance.

Appendix 5

Useful Websites

TELESALES SOFTWARE

Software of the type described in the Case Study at the end of Chapter 2 can be downloaded at the following website: http://www.veritape.com

Note: If you are going to use this software, make sure that:

* you are registered under the Data Protection Act and comply with the requirements of that legislation (see http://www.dataprotection.gov.uk)

* you comply with the law on intercepting and rewording telephone calls (see http://www.dti.gov.uk/cii/regulatory/telecomms/index.shtml – click on 'lawful business practice regulations' – then click on 'Response to consultation' and read Annex B 'Notes for business').

For further information about the Data Protection Act contact the Information Commissioner at Wycliffe House, Waterlane, Wilmslow, Chesire SK9 5AF; Telephone – 01625 545 745 (enquiry line); Email – ringback@dataprotection.gov.uk (you should supply a daytime telephone number).

ALTERNATIVE DISPUTE RESOLUTION

http://www.cedr.co.uk/

ELECTRONIC SIGNATURES

http://www.dti.gov.uk/cii/datasecurity/electronicsignatures/
http://www.tscheme.org/

INSURANCE

http://www.ukinsuranceguide.co.uk/
http://www.theinsurancecentre.co.uk/
http://tiscali.xbridge.com
http://www.tolsonmessenger.co.uk/smallbus.htm

FINDING A LAWYER

http://www.solicitors-online.com/
http://www.legal500.com
http://www.chambersandpartners.com (choose publishing and
then click on 'UK guide')

LATE PAYMENT

http://www.payontime.co.uk
http://www.dti.gov.uk/latepay/index.htm

GOING TO COURT

http://www.courtsservice.gov.uk
http://www.courtservice.gov.uk/mco (Money Claims Online)

OTHER USEFUL BUSINESS SITES WITH LEGAL INFORMATION

http://www.businesslink.org
http://www.ukonlineforbusiness.gov.uk/
http://www.bizzadvice.com/default.asp
http://www.bizwise.co.uk/startup.asp

Note: all website addresses were correct at time of writing but may be subject to change.

Glossary

Alternative dispute resolution (ADR) – an informal procedure for resolving disputes about a contract without having to go to court (see section 14, Chapter 4).

Arbitration – a formal procedure for resolving disputes about a contract without having to go to court (see section 14, Chapter 4).

Assign – assigning a contract means transferring the benefit of the new contract to another person or business. Many contracts restrict the ability of the parties to assign (see section 15, Chapter 4).

Damages – monetary compensation awarded by a court for failure by one party to comply with its legal obligations.

Force majeure – usually refers to acts which are beyond the reasonable control of the parties (see section 13, Chapter 4).

Indemnity – a promise to cover the costs incurred by one party (usually the customer) if certain other promises are not met (usually warranties about the quality of the products or services). (See section 10, Chapter 4.)

Jurisdiction – a jurisdiction is normally a territory in which a particular law applies, e.g. England and Wales (in which English law applies) is one jurisdiction and Scotland (in which Scots law applies) is another. But a court may also 'have jurisdiction' to deal with a dispute even if it relates to something outside that territory. For example, this may be the case if the parties have agreed that English law will apply, even though the agreement relates to business conducted in the US (see section 14, Chapter 4).

Liability – the extent to which one party is legally responsible for failing to do what they promised under a contract or failing to comply with some legal obligation (see section 11, Chapter 4).

Notice – 'giving notice' under a contract means informing the other side that you intend to do something, e.g. terminate the agreement. Most contracts have a formal procedure for giving notice, which often requires a certain amount of advance warning to be given, e.g. one month's written notice (see section 16, Chapter 4).

Party – a person or a business who has signed up to or agreed to certain obligations under a contract (see also 'third party' below).

Recitals – wording at the beginning of a contract which usually sets out the background to the deal (see section 3, Chapter 4).

Risk – responsibility for covering the costs of loss or damage to the goods (see section 8, Chapter 4).

Subcontract – subcontracting means delegating certain of your responsibilities under a contract to another person or business. Many contracts restrict the ability of the parties to do this (see section 15, Chapter 4).

Term – depending on the context, could mean either (i) a provision of the contract; or (ii) the length of the contract. If (ii), (see chapter 3 and section 12, Chapter 4).

Termination – terminating a contract means bringing it to an end (see section 12, Chapter 4).

Third party – a person or a business who is not a party to your agreement. For example, in a contract for supply of hi-fi equipment, the parties to the contract will normally be the supplier and the customer. Third parties could be anyone ranging from the manufacturer of the equipment (assuming someone else makes it) to the customer's customers.

Title – ownership of products or other property (see section 8, Chapter 4).

Warranty – normally a promise that the products or services will meet a particular standard (see section 10, Chapter 4).

Index